COCKTAILS
and
CAMELS

COCKTAILS
and
CAMELS

by
Jacqueline Carol

Appleton-Century-Crofts, Inc.   New York

To
a very special little girl
who believes Mummies can
do anything

Contents

COCKTAILS
and
CAMELS

1

Alexandria—The Melting Pot

I USED TO LIVE IN ALEXANDRIA—EGYPT, THAT IS, NOT AS SOME
Americans think, the one in Virginia.

I liked Alexandria. There was no place like it on earth, I
used to think, and now, on looking back, I am quite sure
there wasn't.

It was a nice, friendly little town basking in the sunshine
and cool Mediterranean breeze, and in summer its streets
smelled of jasmin which little Arab boys sold threaded into
necklaces. Alexandria had plenty of character—characters,
rather—Italian, French, Maltese, Turkish, even White
Russian, to say nothing of Copts, Pashas, Effendis, and bird-
brained but so devoted Sudanese servants. The grocers were
Greek, the jewellers were Jews, the shoemakers were Armenians, and the Lebanese were everywhere. The British
Army used to play polo and complain about the heat. How
they came to be there at all when they had a most roomy
Empire in which to exercise is a long, sad story. For the
British, though they like to look like good-natured and
paternal fools, are, as every Arab knows to his sorrow, very
cunning indeed, especially when it comes to taking advantage of trusting Arabs.

But let's get back to the Lebanese, those charming, hos-

1

pitable people who lived in little villas of twelve bedrooms, threw intimate dinner parties for sixty, and talked so softly that they could be heard in Peru.

Grandmother, Father's mother, a beautiful green-eyed woman with clear white skin and jet-black hair, had come from Damascus at the age of thirteen to marry Grandfather, whom she had never so much as set eyes on before, and because she had been so young and so scared, she had thrown up in the middle of the wedding ceremony.

Grandfather had originated in the Lebanon, when Syria and Lebanon were part of the Ottoman Empire, and after studying in Paris he had emigrated to Egypt and became a prosperous merchant. Ottoman influence in Egypt was almost non-existent by the beginning of the twentieth century.

Although Grandmother had never been to school at all, she could speak five languages fluently and converse intelligently on any number of topics, but she knew a woman's place, and with proper decorum always left the talking in front of strangers to her husband. Behind the scenes, however, it was often she who offered sound advice, for she was a shrewd and capable businesswoman. In spite of the fact that to all intents and purposes the marriage was one of convenience, as marriages so often were in those days, it seems to have worked out very well, for my grandparents had eight boys.

Mother and Father were less fortunate. They had us—three daughters.

Having a daughter was not only nothing to write home about, it was something one should definitely not write home about, and as for having three daughters, it was a calamity and obviously meant that someone had given Mother and Father the Evil Eye.

The Evil Eye was, like the British, very active in the Middle East, and was responsible for everything. If someone admired your new dress and then you spilled coffee all over it, it wasn't that you were a clumsy clot, it was the "Evil Eye," and if your felucca got stuck in some bulrushes which had been there, you knew, since the time of Moses, it had nothing to do with poor seamanship; it was the Evil Eye.

But if Father was disappointed at having three daughters, he never showed it. Indeed, Father never showed anything, for he was not very demonstrative. He was a man of few words, but he thought much, which was very smart of him but most un-Lebanese. Anyway, he faced the fact that he had three daughters very well, far better than Maha, the old Lebanese nanny who had been with Mother before she was married.

Maha was a big moon-faced woman with large brown velvet eyes and pierced ear-lobes from which hung tiny blue beads which were meant to ward off the Evil Eye. She seemed to have been put together out of a series of cushions, making her look something like a Michelin advertisement. I remember that she was very comfortable to sit on. Because she was flat-footed, but mainly because she was Lebanese, she liked to pad around the house and garden in bedroom slippers which she had turned down at the back. Her elephantine tread was always accompanied by the gay jingling of the bunch of keys which hung from her belt and the soft clinking of the thin gold bracelets on her plump wrists. They were her entire fortune and she added one whenever she had saved some money.

Once a week, when she went out on her afternoon off, she painted her eyes crudely with kohl and stuffed herself desperately into a corset and high-heeled shoes several sizes too small for her. Then, pirouetting clumsily in front of us, she'd say, smiling naively like a child, "I'm not all that fat, am I, my darlings?"

"No, no, of course not," we'd say, thinking all the while that we'd never seen anyone so huge in all our lives.

It was always with an evident sigh of relief that she took off her fineries when she came home in the evening and once again put on her beloved sloppy slippers.

Maha had carefully prepared for the arrival of the first child who was to be named after Father's father. She had stitched masses of little blue things not only before Mother was married but before Mother was even engaged. When I arrived, one miserably windy khamseen day in March, she put them all away and sobbed for a week. She did not throw her arms up in the air and cry joyfully, "*Mabrouk, mabrouk,* congratulations, congratulations, may the little one live to be one hundred," and then run down to the kitchen and bake some very special Lebanese dish which would sit on our stomachs for the rest of the night. She did not utter one single little *mabrouk,* for she had to be very careful in her use of the word *mabrouk. Mabrouks* were only used for everything under the sun, everything, that is, except girls— happy things like boys, of course, and really important things like having a new dress or getting over a corn on the foot. But having a girl was not a corn on the foot, it was a pain in the neck. And as for being a girl—well, maybe one could live it up in England or the States, but in the East it was something to live down.

4

"*Maalish*—never mind," Maha finally managed to say philosophically when she had exhausted all her supply of tears. "The next one will be *the boy*. This one is just one of those things."

But it turned out, all because of the Evil Eye, to be three of those things, for the next one was Yvonne and the third, Helen. Maha was distraught with grief. She was a Maronite Catholic and very religious, and she invoked all the saints, especially St. Anthony, with whom she bargained regularly. She even put bread and salt out on a plate for months, which, as everyone knows, is meant to keep the Evil Eye away. But it brought no change, only the ants.

Our house, away from the center of town, overlooked the Mediterranean. It was modern but not screamingly so, and a little too large perhaps to be really cozy, but the rooms were light and airy and very pleasant to live in. The cool sea breeze blew into them and winter sunshine poured through. Virginia creeper had covered most of the façade, and here and there were trails of honeysuckle and jasmin which we threaded into necklaces. There were green shutters, and balconies and verandahs with gay boxes of geranium which contrasted well with the rough gray stucco walls. There were flame trees in the garden, and bougainvillia running wild over the rustic garden gate and splashes of color everywhere. Sweet peas grew high against the wall which separated us from our neighbors, and up the front steps leading to the house were pots of dahlias, carnations, and ferns. Mimosa, mangoes, long-stemmed roses, arum lilies, and nasturtiums—they all grew well in Egypt, and the neighboring gardens were just as prolific.

Our gardener was called Mohamed, after the Prophet.

Tall and thin, he was of a deep brown color like chocolate, and it was difficult to tell his age. He might have been thirty, forty, fifty even. He didn't know. Every morning, soon after dawn, after he had walked from his home by the murky Mahmoudieh Canal, I would hear his footsteps crunching along the garden path beneath my window and into the wooden hut at the bottom of the garden. There he'd take off his shoes, which he sometimes wore on the wrong feet, put on a floppy white hat, and reappear dragging the hose to water the plants before it got too hot.

Five times a day he washed his hands and feet under the garden tap and, on the lawn, prayed towards Mecca, his forehead every now and again bending low to the ground, for he was a devout man and a good Moslem. He never turned a beggar away, and though he could ill afford it, always gave a few piastres from his own pocket. Every year, too, he faithfully observed the month of Ramadan, fasting from sunrise to sunset, taking not so much as a sip of water, even though he worked in the hot sun all day. It was the wealthier, supposedly more educated ones who disregarded their religion, ate pork and drank wine, and turned away the poor.

Mohamed could read and write, for he had taught himself, and when Maha, who could do neither, for she had never been to school, received a letter from her brother up in their native village of Djezzine in the Lebanon, she'd take it to him, holding it straight out in front of her with both hands as though it were something of infinite value. They'd sit under the mimosa tree, Maha overflowing her chair, sipping a little cup of Turkish coffee with great noisy

6

draughts, and Mohamed sitting cross-legged on the grass beside her.

He read slowly and monotonously, going back over the same passage several times, and he held the letter very close to his eyes. It was amazing how many read like that in Egypt.

This simple procedure of receiving a letter was to Maha a very special event. Weeks later, when she had prepared in her mind what she wanted to say to her brother, she and Mohamed would again be under the mimosa tree. It was an elaborate affair. Together, they brought out a wicker table and two chairs which Maha dusted carefully before they sat down. Then she put one sheet of paper, one envelope, and one purple pencil in front of Mohamed. Very carefully, very laboriously, after having moistened the pencil on his tongue, his face distorted with effort, he began to write, "My dear, beloved, respected brother."

Sometimes, his eleven-year-old son Ibrahim came and looked on. Unlike his father, Ibrahim did not wear the local outfit, baggy trousers with the thousand folds and sash at the waist, but European dress—a coarse white cotton shirt and trousers which had been crudely cut down for him.

Ibrahim went to school and could read and write as well as speak a few words of English. None of the other servants were literate, except Hanna, the charming, crooked Lebanese cook.

We kept pigeons and rabbits and chickens, too, and a floating population of lambs and turkeys which resided contentedly on our front lawn and nibbled the grass. These were gifts to Father for Christmas or Sham-el-Nessim. This is the big spring holiday which literally means "sniffing the breeze," when the whole of the local population turns out in its gaudiest colors and squats in Nouzha Gardens eating peanuts. Though these gifts were originally intended for the dinner table, Yvonne, Helen, and I couldn't bear to eat them, and their days of liberty were prolonged almost indefinitely.

Apart from the goldfish in the sun-drenched nursery, there were also tortoises, canaries, a very tired old donkey, and the pick of the ugliest mongrels in the land. Added to the list were the marauders, wild, long-legged cats who came over the garden wall, especially at twilight. A sudden rustle in the bushes, piercing miauls, and we would know that another pigeon had met its doom. In a flash, the whole menagerie was awake. The dogs barked, the donkey brayed, the lambs bleated. The luckless hens, each imagining no doubt that she was to be the next victim, fluttered up and down the coop clucking in panic. Sometimes, if it was not too late, we all made an expedition into the garden. The torch's beam would catch one of the raiders. Crouched in the fork of a tree, it glared back at us with luminous green eyes. How I hated cats.

Alexandrians lived in a comfortable little world of their own, and whatever ups and downs others were having abroad merely went in one ear and out the other. It was difficult to get very excited about events in Europe and America when it did not affect one, when life in Alexandria was pleasant and easy and the shops overflowed with merchandise from the four corners of the earth.

How far away the rest of the world seemed, sitting lotus-eating on the beach with the sun pouring into one's brain, numbing it, or doing the nightly rounds of cocktail parties. Most of the people we associated with were quite content to live and let live, not only where the outside world was concerned, but at home, too. Far better to leave politics, crises, and palace intrigues to the professionals, for politics was an unwholesome hobby and was sometimes apt to cost one's head.

So no one paid much attention to the rumblings both near and far, and the palmy days passed smoothly by, with the only problem of immediate vital interest being what to wear at tomorrow's cocktail party.

In our own immediate circle, the routine of the house ran smoothly, but nothing ran more smoothly than the performance we sat through every evening as we finished dinner, when Hanna the cook came in to do the accounts.

Hanna had come from the Lebanon as a young man when that country was a Turkish province. He hated the Turks and had left to seek a fortune in Egypt. Although he was an excellent cook, he hadn't been very successful at making money, for his one passion in life was playing the horses. In spite of the fact that he was usually in debt, he was gay and debonair, wearing his chef's cap at a jaunty angle. He was plump and smooth, and he would have looked well in top hat and tails, but when one glanced down at his feet, his big toe stuck out of the front of his felt slippers and his socks needed darning at the heels.

Apart from gambling, his only other interest was singing a rather dubious version of "La Madelon," which he had somehow picked up along the way.

The last unprintable words of the song would die away as Hanna entered the room. He'd put his dirty old account book and well-chewed pencil in front of Father. We had discovered long ago that Father was the only one who could

9

match him, and it was a duel as to who could outwit the other. Mother would look down at the cloth and pick up non-existent crumbs. Mrs. James, the English governess, would say, "Don't forget to translate for me, dear," and Yvonne, Helen, and I would settle down to the evening performance.

Father would start to add up, "Milk, lemons, meat, figs, eggs, lemons . . ." and he'd say, "You've put lemons down twice," and Hanna would say "Where?" Father would show him and Hanna would reply that those were the lemons he forgot to put down two days ago, and Mrs. James would ask, "What did the wretched man say?" and I'd translate.

Father, never one to let sleeping dogs lie (or anything else for that matter), would look up the accounts of two days ago and, sure enough, find lemons. Just as he thought. This was flagrant. All cooks made a little here and there, but not everywhere. What did Hanna take him for? An imbecile? He wanted to know.

Mother would pat his sleeve, saying, "Never mind, never mind, Dear," to cover up for the fact that Hanna hadn't answered Father about the imbecile part, and she'd start to pick up crumbs like mad, but Father would glare at Hanna and say very loudly, "You put lemons down two days ago."

Mrs. James hadn't said anything for three seconds, which was an all-time record, so she'd say, "What was that, what was that? Quick, Dear, do translate." And I'd answer, "He said he put lemons down two days ago." "Oooh, did he really! He's just as bad as that man in the West Indies."

But Hanna was quite unruffled. This was no first night. The show had been going on for years with considerable success. So very bored, tilting his cap onto his eyes, he crossed his arms and inspected the ceiling. He answered casually that those were different lemons which Ahmed, the old kitchen boy, had bought.

Ahmed was half-time and half-wit and claimed to be ninety-five or thereabouts, but he looked about fifty. He tottered when he walked and he stuck his neck out. There was a wart on the side of it which Ahmed exercised regularly by pulling out and letting snap again like elastic. His features were soft and gentle, his eyes were bleary, and his mouth always hung open in an imbecilic smile.

At Father's request, he appeared. He smiled daftly and exercised his wart. Father and Hanna both fired their questions at Ahmed loudly and simultaneously.

"Did you buy lemons two days ago?" bellowed Father.

"Don't you remember buying lemons two days ago?" screamed Hanna.

But all Ahmed answered was, "How are you Mazmazell Jacqueline? And you Mazmazell Yvonne? And Mazmazell Helen?"

We answered that we were all very well, thank you. Ahmed was one of our favorites. But unfortunately, Ahmed was not so well tonight.

"*Shufti*—look, my poor arm," he said. "I can only move it up to here." This was right up to the wart. "I'm a very old man. I'm ninety-five, but *maalish,* Allah is merciful, though I have nine daughters."

"Did you buy . . . "

"Good evening, Mrs. Jeeemes, are you good?"

"I'm very well, thank you, Ahmed. Isn't he a dear man?" she said.

"Allah be praised," said Ahmed.

11

Father was about to explode. "Did you or did you not buy lemons?" But Ahmed wasn't through yet. He turned to Mother to ask after her mother's health. Well, it seemed she was better, and Ahmed would say "Allah be praised" again, and Mother, who by this time had not only picked up all the crumbs, but had also picked a few holes in the tablecloth, would decide this was the perfect moment to ask Ahmed how the new twins were. Ahmed, still smiling daftly, would answer that the boy had died, and that he now had eight girls, or was it nine? But *maalish,* it was the will of Allah, and he was ninety-eight and did Mother have any old clothes. Mother never had any old clothes because she gave them away so fast, but she'd find something by tomorrow.

"May Allah bless you, Madam," Ahmed said over and over again, his hands outstretched. "May Allah bless His Excellency as well. (Father was not titled, but it sounded good.) And the house and garden, and all the animals and Mrs. Jeeemes. May you all live to be one hundred."

"I'm going to get to the bottom of this," said Father, and while Mother dabbed her eyes, he and Hanna continued to fire questions at Ahmed.

Ahmed could remember buying bones for the dog, biscuits, and soap, and he'd gone out into the garden to pick one of those loofahs off the tree to scrub the kitchen sink, or was it the dog? He scratched his head. But by Allah, he was ninety-nine and Allah had given him nine daughters ... The angrier Father became, the more he could remember everything except lemons.

By this time, Hanna was muttering to himself about life under the Turks—which he said was bliss compared to life

12

under Father; his horse, which failed even to start, the son of a dog; and advising anyone who cared to listen that we should eat lots and lots of lemons because they were the best thing for the liver.

A jingling of keys told us that Maha too had joined the party. She wanted to know what was going on—as though she didn't know—she had been with the family longer than I had. Gamal, the *suffragi* or servant, made weird sounds sucking his teeth and sliding round and round the table, picking up odd knives and forks and putting them down again in exactly the same place. He wasn't going to leave the room and miss anything.

And if it was a warm night and the windows were open, Mother would worry and say, "Please close the windows, the neighbors will hear us," and Father would reply that he hoped they would, so that they would stop envying us our wonderful cook.

The show usually lasted about thirty minutes, after which the two main characters retired exhausted. The theme was always the same, only the dialogue varied. Sometimes, Hanna charged for something no one could read, not even himself, but he was quite sure we had eaten it. Sometimes, he made a duplicate key and raided the larder and then blamed the rats. Occasionally, Father would infuriate Hanna by bringing home fruits and vegetables which he had bought for a song off a donkey cart on the way back from the office, and he'd exhibit them on the dining room table. He'd challenge Hanna to show off his wares, too, and the two of them would argue the merits of their respective purchases like a couple of village fellaheen.

With the table in front of him groaning under the weight

13

of California apples, Jaffa oranges, and Ismailia melons, and with Hanna to battle with, it was one of the few occasions when Father, a serious and sometimes rigid person, ever seemed to let go and really enjoy himself.

Day in and day out, there was the pantomime with Hanna, and day in day out, as it had done for centuries, the old Nile, without whose life-giving waters all Egypt would be a desert, flowed placidly on to the sea, carrying its burden of cotton bales, feluccas, and dead babies.

2

The Annual Flight out of Egypt

IT WAS PLEASANT TO LIVE IN ALEXANDRIA, WITH ITS WELCOME sea-breeze, its beach-studded Corniche or sea front, which at night resembled a string of pearls, and its green Sporting Club in the middle of the town, where one could practice almost any sport amid a profusion of caddies and ball-boys.

At the Royal Yacht Club by Ras-el-Tin Palace, it was good to make one's way unhurriedly through a delicious meal served by a fleet of suffragis, smart and well-trained, while immediately below lay the harbor, very blue, dotted with a multitude of assorted funnels, masts, and sails.

The drive home, at that wistful hour when the bats come out to play, was perhaps the most memorable of all. The sky would be streaked with every shade from pink to purple, and the shabby, insipid buildings overlooking the Corniche would, for a brief moment, be clothed in gold. The sun dipped into the water like a flaming orange and everything suddenly disappeared into deep blue-gray shadow. There was hardly any twilight. Darkness came quickly, and the moon, if it was full, would rise slowly like an overripe grapefruit and the light clouds passing it would change to yellow. It was often bright enough to read by.

It was pleasant, too, to hear the tinkling of the gharry bell alongside the shiny American car, in the back of which the fat pasha contentedly sat, and ride the upper deck of the clean blue-and-white tram as, to the shrill, almost comic toot of the conductor's whistle, it swayed leisurely past stations with such stirring names as Cleopatra and Camp de Cesar.

In winter, after a brisk walk along the Corniche, with the sea foaming at the mouth with rage from being kicked about by the wind, it was pleasant to have tea at the Beau-Rivage Hotel. Or maybe even a drink downtown at Pastroudis. Or one could drive out to Mariout, about forty minutes from Alexandria, and come back laden with bunches of bright desert flowers.

Alexandria was the foremost port of Egypt, and a hive of activity for the country's cotton brokers, but it was neither a typically Eastern town nor was it altogether European, though a large European community lived there. Except for the poorer sections in and around the harbor area, it was a clean and uncrowded little city, with wide streets flanked by palms and flame trees, large gardens, stylish villas, neat new buildings, and above all, room to breathe.

Life was easy. Labor was cheap. Nothing was impossible, especially when it involved one's comfort. You could have a film developed the same day, a suit made to measure in a matter of hours, a garment invisibly darned for a couple of piastres, and anything you wished copied from a magazine by a host of skillful little artisans for next to nothing. Life, from every point of view, was therefore pleasant—pleasant, that is, until the Cairenes appeared on the scene.

The Cairenes had about as much love for the Alexandrians as the Montagues for the Capulets, yet, every summer, like a swarm of locusts, deserting the dusty, choking heat of Cairo, they swooped down onto Alexandria, avid for the cool city which they made fun of during the rest of the year.

They came spilling out of the trains, packed in the open wagons, in between, on top, while their cars and buses raced frantically down in their haste to get to the sea.

They came, all of them, with their untidy picnic baskets and their bedding—the government clerks and their portly wives, the shrill mothers-in-law covered with fat and cheap jewelry, the well-fed pashas twiddling their amber beads, the cooks, nannies, and suffragis—and they all settled on the beaches so that there wasn't an inch of sand to be seen.

At night, the locusts donned long white sharkskin jackets and invaded the restaurants, open-air cinemas, and casinos, and the only thing for the unfortunate Alexandrian to do was to pack his bags, and, with his Cadillac and his English governess, take the first ship to Europe.

High up on the Jungfrau, or in the Dolomites, it was quiet and peaceful. There wasn't a Cairene in sight—only a few cows—but there was half of Alexandria.

"Chérie!" they'd cry to one another in surprise, in that pure Alexandrian accent of theirs, even though they had come over on the ship together. "What brings you here, Chérie?" The answer was always the same, "I'm running away from those dreadful Cairenes."

Summer seemed to come round very quickly, and before we knew it, it was time once again for the annual flight out of Egypt. There were no exit visas, no travel restrictions of any kind. Most of these came with the Palestine War of 1948.

17

Mother, Yvonne, Helen, the governess, and I usually went on ahead, and Father joined us later, bringing the car with him, and we'd motor wherever the fancy took us. One year, we left without a governess but we took Maha instead. Maha loved Europe and she talked to everyone she came across, first in Arabic, which she was very shocked to find no one could understand, then in atrocious French which no one could understand either, except Helen, who didn't really speak French.

It was a great advantage to be able to rattle away in Arabic without anyone understanding. Unfortunately, there were a few exceptions, like the time in the bus at Cortina d'Ampezzo when Helen asked to change places with me because the old hag on her right smelled, and the old hag turned round and told her in perfect Arabic that she was a very rude little girl.

What seemed to amaze the inhabitants of those countries we visited was the fact that we could speak their language or understand enough to get by. At home, we spoke French, Arabic, and English, as did the majority of our friends. Everyone spoke at least three languages fluently and had perhaps a smattering of another three. Being able to speak several languages without any apparent effort was something we who lived in Egypt took for granted. Yet we belittled ourselves. If a Britisher managed to say three words in unintelligible French after he had lived in France for twenty years, Alexandrians hailed him as a genius and threw a cocktail party in his honor.

On our travels, we always left very early in the morning to get a good start, though the only thing we had to catch was our own car. This was Father's idea and a pretty poor one at that.

Father was an early riser. In fact, Father never went to bed. Instead, he fixed bells and things that didn't need fixing, hammered a few nails into the wall, and walked about the house with special spiked shoes. He never slept at all except at the cinema or when Mother put the radio on. However, at 4 A.M. at the latest, we had to look sharp and be ready to hit the road. He'd wake the concierge, who was supposed to wake us, and then he'd bang on our door as though we had overslept like Sleeping Beauty. "How can you still be asleep at this hour?" he'd cry, aghast.

Sometimes, he banged on a few other doors by mistake, and half the hotel would be up and about. Mother would run around hunting for her handbag, which contained her "essentials"—things like photographs of her eldest sister as a baby, lying on a cushion, dribbling—and which she eventually discovered was on her arm the whole time. The porters, spurred on by Father, carried suitcases downstairs before we had time to close them properly, and half the contents would spill onto the floor. Maha would scream at them in Arabic and then in French, which to the porters and everyone else except Helen was exactly the same thing, and while she invoked St. Anthony, she'd forget all about his little icon which she always kept under her pillow, and she'd only remember it halfway down the other side of the Grossclockner. Then she'd burst into tears and warn us of all the dreadful things that would happen to us if we did not go back and fetch St. Anthony immediately, so naturally, back we'd go, and Yvonne, Helen, and I would be carsick all over again.

19

But it was exciting to see new places and find out how the natives lived in the European jungle. It seemed to me at the time far more of a thrill to go up the Eiffel Tower than the Pyramids, for the West stood for glamour, and the East, no matter how exotic to a European, was to us just home. A great many of our friends had never seen the Valley of the Kings at Luxor, for instance, though they had lived in Egypt all their lives, but they had been to the Riviera dozens of times and had seen the Louvre.

Nobody paid much attention to us until they found out we came from Egypt. But as soon as the word got around, they dropped everything and ran around screaming "the Egyptians are coming," and "the Egyptians are leaving," as though we were Pharaoh's armies. They'd glue their noses to the license plate on the car as though they were studying hieroglyphics, and everyone suddenly seemed to have a passion for collecting Egyptian stamps, but after a while they'd settle down to asking a few sensible questions, such as, did we know a man called Smith—or was it Brown?—who was in India.

Even the little maid up in the hotel at Gstaad, who had been happily going about her work, suddenly became obsessed when she learned that we lived in Egypt. After that, every evening as she turned down the sheets, she implored Mother to take her to Egypt. She wanted, she said, when her day's work was done, to look at a mummy—other than Mother—and sit on the Pyramid which she was quite convinced rose in our back garden.

One day, Mother was sitting in the lounge of a hotel in Budapest (surely one of the most beautiful cities in the world) when two middle-aged American women rushed up and, pointing to her, squealed excitedly, "Eee-gypt! The hall porter says you come from Egypt! Oh, do tell us about those glorious, romantic sheiks of yours."

Mother was so taken aback, she couldn't say a word. "Take it easy, Ethel," said one. "The poor thing obviously only speaks Bedouin language. Such a tiny little Bedouin, isn't she? But," she added, quite satisfied, "a real one. Let me speak to her." She bent down so that her nose almost touched Mother's.

"We're Americans." As though anyone within ten miles had any doubts. "America. Bay City, Michigan. We're just dying to hear about your exciting sheiks."

"Sheeks?" Mother echoed.

"She's trying to understand," cried the one called Ethel.

"Isn't she darling?" cried the other. "What's your name, little Bedouin lady? I'm Mildred and this is Ethel. We're traveling round the world playing the piano. At least, I'm the pianist and Ethel sings. Some people say we are crazy but we are really artistes."

And then Father came up and said, *"Qui sont ces deux folles?"* and explained rather tactlessly that sheiks were very worthy gentlemen who bore not the slightest resemblance to Rudolph Valentino. Naturally, they wouldn't believe this, and kept repeating: "But don't their eyes flash? But don't their eyes flash?" Father was adamant. He wouldn't admit to being a Bedouin, not even though Mother implored him, for the sake of Michigan—and he didn't live in an oasis in the middle of the Sahara. What's more, he'd never spent a night under a tent in his life. He did, however, suggest that Ethel and Mildred join us for a drink and perhaps perform for us afterwards. They did. And it was a riot, with

21

half the people in the hotel running down to see who had been murdered. We also learned many interesting things about the natives of Bay City, Michigan.

One of the most unusual and interesting people we met on our prewar holidays was Howard Carter, who discovered the tomb of Tut-ankh-Amen in the Valley of the Kings at Luxor. It was up in the hotel at St. Moritz and I was only twelve at the time, but as it so often is with childhood memories, it seems like yesterday.

Every evening on their way to the dining room, the hotel guests were drawn as though by a magnet to the slot machine where, with one franc and a good deal more luck, a crane would reach down amongst a multitude of bonbons and come up not with bubble gum but with silver cigarette boxes and Swiss watches. Howard Carter would invariably be there with a bagful of one-franc pieces, much determination, and a rare stock of fabulous magic phrases which no doubt had lain dormant for four thousand years.

"Abracadabra, you stupid thing," he'd chant soothingly at first. "Abracadabra, hashamatasha, wooloo, wooloo, wooloooo." Then, as the crane came up with only a handful of sweets, he'd use some rather un-Pharaonic words and put in another franc.

Angrily now, he'd cry, "Abracadabra, abracadabra, hashamatasha, wooloo, wooloo, wooloooo." With the crane about to land half an inch away from a silver cigarette case, Carter, who was a strong man, would shake the slot machine, unhinging it from the wall. The crane swerved, landed on its object, and with some more magic words, the cigarette case would drop into the waiting receptacle.

"Here you are," he'd say to anyone who happened to be

standing by. "You take it. Now let's have a crack at that lighter there."

Then, after dinner, Mrs. James, our memorable governess, would, in her own irresistible way, kidnap him and bring him over to sit with us. He was a most entertaining person. Though we did not like to press him to tell us the story of his discovery of the Tut-ankh-Amen tomb, the subject naturally arose.

I can still vividly remember his telling us of the awe he felt when, after having fruitlessly excavated for months, he looked through a hole into the antechamber of the tomb, by the light of a candle flickering in the warm air that was escaping, and saw, as though through a mist, statues, alabaster, and gold everywhere. Some four thousand years had passed since human feet had stood on that same spot where he and his friend the Earl of Carnarvon made their dramatic discovery. Then, as his eyes grew accustomed to the darkness, he could pick out beautiful individual objects. It must have been an amazing and magnificent sight to look into that tomb which, unlike the others in the Valley of the Kings, was almost intact.

It seemed so strange to hear the story of Tut-ankh-Amen told us by an Englishman some five thousand feet high in the mountains of Switzerland.

Mother always maintained that traveling was an education in itself, and that if we missed a few days of school—it usually stretched to several months—at the beginning and end of term, we would more than make up for it with all the things we had picked up along the way. She was not only referring to governesses, which we imported and deported at a fantastic rate, and autographs of celebrities, most of

23

whom became nobodies. For when, in school, Yvonne, who was as bright as she was good-looking, was asked what had struck her most about Switzerland, she was able to answer without a moment's hesitation that it was the sense of humor.

By the first week of October, the last Cairene had returned to the capital, and for the Alexandrians, too, the seasonal migration was over. We were glad to be going back to Egypt. Europe was all very well for a holiday and next year, no doubt, we'd be delighted to see it again, but the way I looked at it, there was no place like Alexandria in the whole world.

Once again we were leaning over the rail of the *S.S. Ansonia,* watching the low, pale yellow outline of Alexandria come into focus. The pilot's launch flitted lightly across the water, the green flag with its crescent and three stars flying in the wind, and soon the pilot was climbing up the rope ladder followed by the port authorities and a few unmilitary looking *chaouiches,* or policemen, in white uniforms and red fezzes.

Father took our passports and went into the dining room, which had been cleared of all the tables and assigned for the disembarking formalities. Suddenly, all hell seemed to break loose. People who had been happily gazing at the approaching coastline began to rush up and down the decks shouting in every known language, gesticulating, shoving, sweating, cursing, endeavoring to get their passports stamped and be the first down the gangway. But all was well. It was always like that.

The pashas and the privileged ones never needed to attend to the passports themselves. Out of nowhere, there always appeared some little man, fawning and unshaven, who would battle his way through and shout himself hoarse

24

for His Excellency the Pasha. And all for a few piastres. Meanwhile, His Excellency the Pasha waited in the lounge and ordered another cup of coffee, for even in the midst of a tornado, there was always time for Turkish coffee.

There was the familiar harbor scene again. The Yacht Club and its jetty, around which clustered gleaming white yachts and dinghies and the handful of motorboats belonging to some of the wealthier Alexandrians. Nearby, the lighthouse.

Yvonne and I had been up in it once with our governess, a Miss Shelby, who wore transparent blouses and not much else, and whose boy friend was somehow all tied up with the lighthouse. He had told us about Pharos, which he said had been one of the Seven Wonders of the World, but the way he had looked at Yvonne, she was obviously the eighth, and Miss Shelby had never taken us again.

A couple of British warships were sending out signals and shrill whistles, and on the deck of one of them, sailors still in white uniforms were putting up flags and bunting. There was probably a cocktail party on board tonight. Several British destroyers were scattered all around as well, for since the recent Anglo-Egyptian Treaty of 1936, the Royal Navy had been granted the right to use Alexandria Harbor for a period of eight years.

"Isn't it a beautiful day?" the new governess always asked.

People always talked about the weather in Europe; we never did in Egypt. It was just there, taken for granted like anything else.

"It's always a beautiful day in Egypt," Mother would say. "Wait till you've seen the winters."

The quayside grew nearer and nearer, and with it the

25

loud roar of voices. Slowly, the ship docked alongside and the gangway was finally lowered. The noise from the dining room became hysterical as passengers and fawning little men made one last spurt round the green baize-covered table where the officials sat examining papers and passports.

On the quayside itself, a mass of galabias—the long robes worn by most of the very poor Arabs—and red fezzes shouted and waved handkerchiefs. It was as though the ship was floating in a sea of brown faces. You could almost touch them. You could almost smell them, and the noise was deafening. Sleek new cars and withered old taxis inched their way through the crowd, honking their horns in long intermittent gasps, and a group of ragged-looking men, ropes tied round their middles, chanted monotonously in refrain as they hauled an enormous crate away from the ship. The sun, beating down with its usual fire, couldn't find a single cloud to hide its blushing face.

At the bottom of the gangway, a couple of luckless policemen tried to keep order and restrain the crowd, but they were having a hard time. One policeman, the corners of a checkered handkerchief showing under his fez to keep the sweat from falling into his eyes, was noisily coming to blows with a man selling rugs. The man, with the unshaven look of a badly-plucked fowl and an assortment of rugs draped over one shoulder, screamed at the top of his voice that the whole of the police force were sons of dogs, and that this particular policeman was something quite unprintable.

Having so said, he turned round and raced up the gangway with surprising agility, followed by a swarthy friend completely smothered under a mass of leather bags of every shape and size, painted over with the Pyramids and the

Sphinx. The men had grabbed hold of their galabias between their teeth to enable them to run up faster, but they still managed to scream, "Souvenir, nice souvenir, souvenir, berry good, berry nice." There is no "v" in Arabic and this sound is sometimes found difficult to pronounce.

For a moment, the policeman looked as though he was about to follow them, but he was fat and he was hot, and it was like that every day. He removed his fez, took the handkerchief and mopped his brow, after which he spat into the handkerchief, folded it neatly, and put it into his pocket. Those wretched salesmen. Now they'd be on deck selling that junk to those stupid British and French tourists who would pay twice the value and think what a bargain they were getting. And if they were American, they'd be even more stupid and wonder if they hadn't perhaps robbed the poor old Arab.

He had actually overhead an American couple once, for he could understand a little English. "Joe," the woman had said, "may the good Lord forgive you, you've robbed that poor man."

Poor? Ha! Those salesmen. They made more money than he did. The devil take them.

"There's Mahmoud," cried Helen.

Mahmoud was our driver. He wore a fez, morning coat, and gold teeth. He hadn't seen us, but then he never seemed to see anything anyway, especially when he was driving. Mahmoud was a nice man, but he ran into people. He'd spot a man ambling in the middle of the road, minding his own business—instead, admittedly, of minding where he was going—and he'd make a beeline for him. Having landed him on the hood with a great big thud, Mahmoud continued

27

to drive. He'd take both his hands off the steering wheel because he needed them to talk with and he'd scream at the man at the top of his voice that he was the son of a dog in seven languages. For some mysterious reason, the man would have exactly the same opinion of Mahmoud, and after they had both glued their faces to opposite sides of the windshield, threatening to wipe each other off the face of the earth, they'd suddenly realize they not only knew each other—they were brothers. Then they'd roar with laughter and Mahmoud would stop the car, and both would say *maalish, maalish,* and slap hands noisily and inquire after each member of their respective families in turn, and Mother would sit in the back of the car like a little mouse, hoping that everyone's health would be excellent, because she was in a hurry to get to the Greek grocer's and buy olives.

Father reappeared, hot and weary from the free-for-all over the passports. It was much hotter now that the ship had docked.

"They're down there, all of them," Mother said. "They" were that very same body of relatives and friends who had seen us off three months ago. They had showered us with flowers and kisses and Turkish delight, and brought huge boxes of chocolate which had melted before the ship had even left the harbor.

"Oh, no," said Father, "not all of them. We'll be up all night."

But Mother, who had the real family spirit, said, "It's very nice of them to have come. They must have been standing there for hours."

At last we were coming down: Mother, Father, the governess, Yvonne, Helen, and I, followed by our barefoot and

28

perspiring porters, carrying on their backs the enormous trunks one traveled with in those days of abundance, and we were engulfed and smothered in the tender arms of our affectionate aunts and uncles and cousins. "Yes, Auntie, I had a wonderful time, thank you. Yes, Uncle, I had a wonderful time, thank you. Yes, Cousin, I had a wonderful time, thank you . . . "

We fought our way to the car, Mahmoud leading, a swarm of beggars bringing up the rear. Standing by the car, holding the door open, was Ahmed, the beggar with the wooden leg. We knew him well. He had even come to the hospital, pathetically clutching a bunch of roses, the day Helen had had her appendix out. At first the hospital had refused to let him in, and the receptionist had phoned up to Helen's room and said that "some filthy Arab downstairs" claimed to know her, though of course, he hastened to add, there must be some mistake. But there was no mistake and Helen had been delighted to see him.

Ahmed shooed all the other beggars away, which we hadn't been able to do, and as we piled into the car, he poured forth a string of flowery compliments. They come easily in the Arabic language, and although we did not take them too literally, we felt no pain on hearing that Alexandria had sobbed over our absence, but was now as though illuminated with a thousand lights because we were back. Naturally, Mother gave him all her change.

We drove off followed by the relatives and friends in their cars, all of them trailing us home. Through the paved and narrow streets we went, at a snail's pace, past the filthy, decrepit buildings with their miserable black entrances, and the cheap food shops hung with carcasses of meat black with flies.

Our path was jammed with Arabs clad in galabias and brightly colored pajamas, and barefooted black-veiled women with silver bracelets on their ankles, carrying half the contents of their houses, or so it seemed, on their heads. This never ceased to amaze me, for I couldn't even manage a book without letting it fall.

Quite oblivious of the oncoming car, kids in rags darted across the street, or sat in the middle of it playing marbles with small round stones, or fought each other, wildly shouting obscenities. The licorice man, a striped red apron full of holes across his bulky middle, and a big brass container slung across one shoulder, went about clinking two brass plates together to attract attention, and an old moth-eaten-looking mule unconcernedly ate its clover, which had overflowed onto the pavement.

Mahmoud never took his hand off the horn to warn everyone of impending doom, but it had not the slightest effect. "Sons of dogs, savages," he muttered as he nearly mowed down a youth zigzagging on a gaily festooned bicycle and a couple of women arguing shrilly in the middle of the road.

We left the harbor area and the warm smell of local bread, dust, and filth, and drove through the center of town. The familiar names of the stores were written in European letters—hardly any were in Arabic then—but the stores themselves were closed, for it was still the siesta hour—they would open at four—and the streets were clean and almost deserted.

The Abukir Road, which connected the center of town with the residential area of Ramleh, was a straight wide avenue flanked by palm trees and new constructions, chiefly schools and hospitals, and flowers grew in an orderly fashion down the middle. I hoped the tourists would see this part of Alexandria and not judge the town by the harbor area.

Gradually, the Abukir Road began to lose its formality and, narrowing considerably, proceeded to meander ever so slightly past beautiful old villas and smiling gardens which became more numerous as we went further into Ramleh. Glimpses of smooth, carefully-tended lawns could be caught through some of the fancy wrought-iron gates, and bright red bougainvillia toppled over garden walls.

Shops disappeared altogether except for an occasional grocery store. And suddenly, when you least expected to see it, next door to the most distinctive villa of all, housed in a sprawling, one-story building, was the local café—an institution in itself—where all the cooks and suffragis, drivers, and gardeners with or without jobs congregated.

Marble-topped tables with ugly black legs and crude wooden chairs overflowed onto the pavement where customers in galabias and shabby, unmatching European trousers and jackets sipped Turkish coffee or played a kind of backgammon. You could hear the sharp click of the draught as it was brought down onto the board. Some smoked the narghile.

A Bedouin woman waddled by carrying a child astride her shoulders, and her nails were orange from henna. The men stared hard.

At night, under the garish acetylene lamps hanging from the ceiling, the red fezzes and the white galabias huddled at the tables stood out even more. The café was packed and everyone sat as though drugged by the loud and monotonous, yet fascinating, wail of Arabic music, which, until one learns to like it, sounds like a chorus of suffering cats.

We turned off the Abukir Road, up a very short steep hill with the flame trees meeting overhead, and we were home.

We had already spotted them standing waiting at the garden gate: Gamal, the suffragi, his face very black above his white *uftan,* a kind of galabia; Hanna, the crooked cook whom Father regularly fired once a week; Mohamed, the devout gardener; and Ahmed, the kitchen boy. And like the dean of them all stood Maha, flat feet in sloppy slippers and wearing a bright pink dress with huge daisies on it, for she loved bright colors, which to her seemed like delicate pastel shades. To speed us on our way, she had sent us countless dazzling postcards of cherubs and angels, which Mohamed had written for her. She threw herself on us all, smothering us to death as though we had just managed to return safe and sound from some perilous safari, laughing and crying at the same time. She had an abundance of tears, whether she was happy or sad, or even if the neighbors' nanny had bought some material with larger daisies on it than her own. Maha then turned to Helen, who was her favorite because she ate like a pig and would soon look like her, and asked, as she always did, "Now tell me truthfully, my precious one, which did you prefer, Paris or France?"

By this time, the relatives had arrived and poured out of the cars like marines making a landing, and into the drawing room we went, the blue room for the homecoming, with the distant and not-so-distant aunts and the cousins once, twice, and thrice removed. Would St. Anthony only have removed them all!

Having done with the embracing and the pinching of

cheeks, and the "My, how the girls have grown, ha, ha, ha" (grownups always seem so surprised because children grow) , and the "Do you remember your old Aunt Karima?"—as if anyone could ever forget her, all repeated half a dozen times over, they seated themselves in a large circle. They were all there—Uncle Nessim, who fussed with the ends of his mustache; Grandmother, whose green eyes Yvonne had inherited; Aunt Angèle, who hated the sun and never went out of the house without her flowered cretonne parasol; and Karim, the nice young man next door who was in love with Yvonne. Our respective families were very pleased at the romance, for they had had Yvonne and Karim coupled in their minds since they were children.

The little cups of Turkish coffee were passed round by Gamal, and the talk went on and on, with eyes and hands all taking part in the conversation. Everyone talked at once, because the only person who is interesting is oneself, but one could hear cousin Marie's voice pitched high above the others. It went right through one like a dagger. She looked like a Pekinese with a pearl choker, and she wore long dangling earrings which swayed furiously when she got excited. She was very proud of her son Robert—Title: Eligible Bachelor. She spent her time scanning the horizon through a pair of lorgnettes for a suitable wife for him with all the exigencies of royalty, but no one ever came up to her requirements.

Heavy and balding slightly, Robert sat across the room from her by the vase of arum lilies, deep in his favorite topic of conversation: cotton. It was his be-all and end-all and he talked of nothing else.

Gamal came in softly with a tray of crystallized dates and

rose-petal jam. Father was saying how the Italians, with their heads full of their Ethiopian campaign, had, on seeing the Arabic license plate on the car, taken us for Abyssinians, at the same time as Aunt Karima was telling us the life history of her bladder, which, it seems, was like a straight pipe. Aunt Emilie wanted to know why we hadn't been to the Lebanon and seen all the relatives; after all, one must stick together. And Mother, instead of replying that there were enough right where we were, launched herself into an account of the Swiss doctor who was firmly convinced she reclined on a divan all day sipping syrups and being fanned by slaves. What strange ideas Europeans had of Egypt.

I could hear Yvonne telling Karim how we had met Marshal Pétain (before he went down in infamy) and sat with him at Lausanne watching the little steamers chug across the lake from Evian, and Cousin Marie with the Pekinese face was saying how she envied the girl who would eventually marry Robert, and Cousin Georgette was inviting us to taste her special figs one day soon, dried on her own terrace because the sun there was better than anywhere else in Alexandria, and Gamal appeared again, with some mulberry syrup and cakes from Baudrot's, downtown, because we hadn't eaten anything for at least fifteen minutes and we mustn't appear to be inhospitable.

Grandmother's green eyes looked round the room at all the relatives and came to rest on Aunt Naife, who had fallen asleep, lost in the depths of the big armchair. Aunt Naife, who was nearing a hundred, was quite toothless, and so tiny that her feet didn't touch the ground. Every now and again, she'd wake with a start and say to Mother in her high cracked voice, "When are you going on your holiday? But you must

34

go on a holiday," and Mother would mutter, "Yes, yes, soon," and everyone would look at everyone else as much as to say, "Poor old Aunt Naife, she's not quite all there, and soon she won't be there at all. How sad, poor Aunt Naife."

It was only hours later, when even Grandfather's handsome life-size portrait on the wall seemed to droop a little, that the relatives made a move to leave—to have dinner, they said, though it was nearer breakfast time—and we were able to unpack and wash our faces of the lipstick smears left by our well-meaning but over-affectionate relatives.

It never occurred to me that a homecoming could be any different.

3

Governesses

WE HAD THIRTEEN GOVERNESSES—NOT AT THE SAME TIME, but following closely on one another's heels—and on ours, unfortunately, for nice girls in Alexandria were very strictly chaperoned and were not allowed to take so much as a step on their own. If they did, it was assumed they were up to no good and obviously "not nice." It was only halfway through the Second World War, when—according to the good ladies of Alexandria society—every girl's morals had gone to the dogs, that Yvonne, Helen, and I were even allowed to go to a movie without the governess.

The governesses were of every shape, size, and vintage. They were French and they were English. They were Swiss and they were German. And they were also nuts.

But mostly they were English, for the English governess, now a species almost extinct in Egypt and, I suspect, in other parts of the world, was in full bloom during the middle 1930's. Even if she dropped her "H's" and latched them on when there was no need to, she was still considered very fashionable, very chic, on a par with one's Cadillac and beach house at Sidi-Bishr. She was the governess of kings and queens—indeed, sometimes she thought she *was* royalty.

It was also, unfortunately, thought very smart to speak

English and look down on Arabic, which many people considered only good enough to speak to the servants. With the rise of Arab nationalism, Arabic became more and more in demand, and those who had scorned the language of the country they had lived off for years were to pay heavily for their shortsightedness and arrogance.

But be that as it may, we never moved without the governess, even when we went to Europe for the summer holidays. Sometimes the governess couldn't stand the pace, and sometimes she couldn't stand me, and we'd leave Alexandria with one and return with another.

Mother, who was very shy and terrified of interviewing governesses, could never bear to say "no" when one appeared at the door. The result was that we had women like Fräulein, a big, blond giant built on the lines of a professional wrestler. Father swore Mother had engaged her to move the furniture. Not only was Fräulein in the habit of eating bananas and feeding the skins to Helen, who, besides being three years old at the time, hadn't heard of fair shares for all, she was also partial to singing some native songs which, we discovered the night the German Consul came to dinner, were not only folk but vulgar.

And then there was Miss Halsey, a red-faced Australian who claimed it was much healthier to jump out of the windows of our upper floor, which were well over twenty-five feet high, than use the stairs. We never saw her do this, though we wished she would, but she never failed to dive off the lower balconies and verandahs right into poor Mohamed's beautiful flower beds.

"Come on, you sluggards!" she'd cry. "Shakes you up a bit, what?"

In truth, it shook us all no end.

Maha would curse her in choice Arabic and sneak us up the back stairs to her little room, the walls of which were plastered with pictures of saints, and implore St. Anthony to send Miss Halsey back to the kangaroos. Then, while we gorged ourselves on delicious homemade date jam stuffed with almonds, Maha would tell the same old story of a sultan who really had a problem: whether to break the valuable vase in which his only son had trapped his hand, or whether to cut off the boy's hand. The sultan just wept and wept, and the problem, like many in the Middle East, was never settled.

But the procession of governesses suddenly stopped the day Mrs. James sailed through the revolving doors of the Beau-Rivage Hotel in Lausanne. Our last English governess had run off with a hot- if not blue-blooded Italian count in Florence, and Mother had written to an agency in London to send over—she had especially insisted on this—"someone who would not be seasick, who spoke a foreign language, and who was, in short, a lady."

And they had sent Mrs. James.

"How do you do?" she said. We stared. Mrs. James wore a black velvet cloak lined with purple, and something like a tiara on her head. Helen whispered, "Has she come from the Court of St. James?" and curtsied before I could reply.

Mrs. James said she hoped she hadn't kept us waiting. She had a beautiful accent. Very British, you know. Supper was always at eight in the West Indies, but it wouldn't take her a minute to change. She laughed lightly. She was a lady, you could see that.

She assured Mother that she not only spoke fluent French, but also Italian, Spanish, and Portuguese. She had sailed

round the world not once but twice, and she knew all about
the tropics and being served dinner by natives who wore
nothing but a suntan and a ring through the nose, ha, ha,
ha; oh, dear, isn't the world a funny place? Had we heard
about the Japanese who was asked what had struck him
most about Europeans and had answered the odd shape of
their eyes? And as Christopher Columbus said—he was
British, of course—he said, it's a small world. What? Christopher Columbus? Why, Papa (this to Father), of course
he was British. There is no more British name than Christopher, except perhaps George. Her youngest brother was
Christopher Charles Colin. She remembered his names
because they all begin with a "C." Why, she had even been
through a cyclone in the West Indies, and had drifted on
the Caribbean in a trunk and had sucked the leather of her
boots to keep alive, because, though there was water, water
everywhere, there wasn't a drop to drink. Seasick? What, her?
How hilarious! Why, she didn't know the meaning of the
word.

Mother breathed a sigh of relief. This one would be different. Mother was never so right in her life.

With our newly acquired paragon, we motored to Genoa
to board the Lloyd Triestino ship to Alexandria. Mrs. James
changed clothes so often and was so well dressed that a
couple of times en route it was Mother who was taken for
the governess. But apart from that, it was like every motor-
ing trip we had ever taken.

"You'd better stop, Dear," Mother would say after taking
one look at our faces, and Father immediately jammed on
the brakes—usually in the middle of a hairpin bend—which

precipitated things a little, and Yvonne, Helen, or I would be sick down his neck.

Strangely enough, Mrs. James too was sick, which was disappointing, but she blamed the cold roast beef she had eaten in that restaurant in Milan. She should have had spaghetti like the rest of us, she said. "One never knows what the food is like in those foreign parts." Obviously, it was an accident.

We arrived at Domodossola, the Italian frontier. Confident in their interpreter, Mother and Father, who spoke only a smattering of Italian, ushered forth Mrs. James in front of the customs official, and waited, beaming.

It soon became apparent, however, that in spite of the high-speed gibberish, no progress was being made. We approached and listened to our fluent linguist in action. *"Yo, yo*—no, that's Portuguese. I mean, *prego,"* she was saying, "here are the baggag-lies. Oh, pooh, don't be ridiculous, I'm British. Yes, *si, si,* the name is Penelope Amanthe Ethel James, though I don't see what it has got to do with you."

She then turned to us and said indignantly, "Mama, Papa (for some reason, she never called my parents anything else), the wretched man doesn't speak a word of Italian."

She continued, quite unabashed, *"Prego, prego,* I'm not going to say it again, you know. Oh, you're the limit, you silly little macaroni, you. If I had my own way, I'd give you the back of the brush. Come," she said, turning to us, swinging her cloak round, and led us away.

We boarded the *Esperia,* Mrs. James with head high, then Mother and Father followed by the three of us wearing our habitual green traveling masks.

"Fancy being seasick on a mere three-day voyage," scoffed

Mrs. James, as Yvonne, Helen, and I excused ourselves from the dinnertable, leaving chianti and canelloni untouched. "Why, when I was in the West Indies . . . "

But we had hardly been in our berths a quarter of an hour when we heard someone moaning in the passage outside. The perfect English accent was familiar. Tottering through the doorway came Mrs. James. Gone was the bravado. She clung to the wall, her face the color of hashish, moaning pitifully, "Oh, I'm very sick, oh, I'm so sick," and then a scream, "Call Mama, I'm going to die!"

It took Mama and the stewardess to put Mrs. James to bed. She lay flat on her back with one arm hanging limp over the side of the bunk, moaning continuously, "I'm going to die. I need sustenance. Bring me some Brussels sprouts and bananas. It's the only thing I can keep down."

We were so interested in this strange diet that, for the first time in our lives, we got up and dressed and quite forgot to be sick.

Every hour, the stewardess, who was as fascinated as the rest of us, brought in, panting, a great big tray of sprouts and bananas. Mrs. James would suddenly sit up, swallow the whole thing like one of those American garbage Disposalls, and promptly fall back again, moaning: "I'm going to die," which, considering everything, was not really surprising. "*Mamma mia, la poveretta,*" said the stewardess sympathetically. "I have never seen anything like it."

This was an understatement, the stewardess had never had it so good. It was like Christmas. Mother was tipping her every hour for the sprouts.

Mrs. James moaned like a foghorn and remained horizontal for the rest of the trip, swallowing the last plateful of sprouts to be scrounged on board just as the ship mercifully sailed into Alexandria. Then, suddenly resuscitated, she changed into an elegant outfit we hadn't seen before, put on a smart little white hat with a veil—to keep the flies off, she said—and joined us on deck to greet the East. And the relatives.

When we arrived home, she sat down gracefully in the midst of the aunts and uncles and cousins. "Is she the new governess?" whispered the relatives loudly. They were very impressed with Mrs. James and told her how smart she was.

"Smart? What, this old thing?" laughed Mrs. James, obviously delighted. "Why, I made that out of bits and pieces, bits and pieces, that's all. This is something I picked up in a henhouse in Chile, and you know what this is, of course," pointing to her blouse. "I've had it since the year dot. It's part of an old tablecloth someone gave my great-grandmother."

"Mama, Papa," she continued, hardly pausing to take a breath, "doesn't dear Aunt Naife remind you of my own mother, who is ninety-nine?" That Mama and Papa had never so much as set eyes on Mrs. James' mother was an example of Mrs. James' reasoning at its best. "Of course, she drinks a bottle of Guinness every night. And my daughter," she continued, "takes size nine in shoes, and she is only eight, you know."

Cousin Marie, the Pekinese, asked if Mrs. James ever suffered from seasickness.

Mrs. James drew herself up, "What? Me? Seasick?" She laughed herself silly. "Did I ever tell you what happened to me when I was in the West Indies?"

Before we knew it, she had drifted to the Caribbean in a

trunk and was being served dinner by a native who wore nothing but a suntan and shoelaces. She didn't say where the shoelaces were worn. The family had gone out to dinner, and she had assured the Ambassador that she would be perfectly all right, since she spoke fluent Spanish. "You know the Ambassador, of course," said Mrs. James to everyone in general, as though she was referring to some night club. It didn't matter anyway; the Ambassador had nothing to do with the story.

It seems she wanted some more cheese, so, in the tone a Britisher uses in the tropics to show a native that the native is only a foreigner, she demanded, "*Un poco di beso*," but the wretched man didn't move.

She began to get angry. "*Un poco di beso*," she demanded again, this time more loudly.

"But the wretched man, do you know what the wretched man did?" she asked. "He bent down and kissed me and then ran out of the room. I ask you. After all, *baso, kaso,* or *peso,* it's all the same wretched foreign language."

She went on and on, pouring it out as though it came out of a syphon, while the relatives sat entranced.

"Now, of course," she went on, "you can always tell a lady. Did I ever tell you what happened to me on the tennis court at Wimbledon one day? The semi-finals, or was it the finals? Now, let me see. Semi-finals, that's right. Oh, yes, I've played quite a few games in my time. I was coming up to take a beautiful backhand, when I felt something round my ankles. You'll never guess what it was. Helen dear, little girls should be seen and not heard. Yes, my purple bloomers with the lace. I quickly pulled them off, threw them up in the air, and hit such a beautiful backhand that Coots—that was the

43

American—couldn't get it, and they landed on the apple tree. Helen dear, little girls should be seen and not heard. Why, of course, Wimbledon's just full of apple trees, as we all know who have played there. Oh, dear," she sighed, "that was a memorable day."

I thought, but didn't like to say, that it was a memorable night as well. If she had been playing a magic flute, she couldn't have charmed the relatives more. They were so charmed, in fact, that it looked as though they would be with us for at least a year. They sat, all of them, hardly batting an eyelid, absolutely hypnotized by the sound of Mrs. James' voice.

"Aren't they lovely people," said Mrs. James, when they finally got up to leave. "So interesting. Isn't the East full of fascinating people?"

Well, perhaps it is, I thought, but it occurred to me too that whether East, West, or up the Pole, the most fascinating person to be found anywhere was our new English governess.

Before the war broke out in September, 1939, our house had been relatively quiet—as quiet as it could be, that is, with governesses and chauffeurs all coming and going at once, and our friends dropping in to see our menagerie. But now they came in droves from miles around to see Mrs. James in her heroic role as Florence Nightingale.

It all started with passers-by collecting at the garden gate. At first, we thought it was merely because of their understandable curiosity at seeing Mrs. James ride the old donkey Hashasha sidesaddle, while Ahmed tottered behind it like a drunk with a carrot in his hand.

But we soon realized that they were all falling on a particularly slippery patch of pavement just outside the garden gate. The garden quickly turned into an out-patient department, with Mrs. James flying hither and thither, dishing out coffee, iodine, and stories from the West Indies to all casualties. She said it reminded her of the war in South America. I forget which one.

In the end, Mrs. James got organized and preferred to sit by the gate, hidden by the rhododendron bushes, and wait for the passers-by to fall into her lap. She wore a white scarf round her neck and a clean white apron which she fancied made her look like the matron of the Twelfth General Hospital at Chatby. Pinned to her apron was a brooch, which, if one looked at it carefully, read "Paddock." Her eyes glistened with happy anticipation whenever she heard footsteps coming down the hill. "Aha, aha, I knew it, they're not looking where they are going." She rubbed her hands with glee. "Oops, there they go, three of them," she'd cry, as though she had caught a bagful of grouse, and she'd fling open the garden gate and tell everyone to make themselves comfortable on the lawn, because all she said was *"un poco di beso"* and the wretched man kissed her, and she wouldn't be a minute getting her bandages and instruments, and had they heard about her daughter Francesca who wore size nine in shoes and drank a glass of Guinness every night?

In the meantime, my grandmother, who was ninety if she was a day but who never liked to miss a thing, and who, since we had Mrs. James, visited us almost every day with Aunt Karima of my-bladder's-like-a-straight-pipe fame, shouted at the top of her lungs, "Gamal, Gamal, bring them all mulberry syrup, bring them all mulberry syrup. Gamal, Gamal, don't forget the ice. The *ice*."

It was madly gay. We never had so many people around,

and things got even madder when Afrit, the mongrel, began to bite.

He was a tiny little beast who looked exactly like a rather large rat. When we had found him abandoned in the street as a puppy, his fur had been soft and fluffy, but now it was just like sandpaper. No one ever stroked him.

There was nothing Afrit liked better than to get his sharp little teeth into the calves of the R.A.F. men who happened to pass by. Whenever they passed our gate, which was at least a dozen times a day, Afrit charged like the Light Brigade. There was a brief scuffle, a lot of beautiful R.A.F. language, and Afrit returned from battle with some York ham or English mutton in his mouth. He never looked at home-grown produce.

While Grandmother and Aunt Karima screamed for Gamal to bring the mulberry syrup with the ice, and we and our friends ran around fetching and carrying and adding to the general confusion, Mrs. James, her white scarf flowing in the wind, poured forth floods of iodine and words and mended wounds, trousers, and tempers, after which she added another bit of R.A.F. blue to her collection of "bits and pieces."

4

France Is à la Mode

A FOREIGNER COMING TO EGYPT BEFORE THE SECOND WORLD War may have been surprised to find the French language so widely spoken and French customs so prevalent. Many of the wealthier Egyptians and Syrians (Syrians generally meant Syrians and Lebanese) had been educated at Jesuit colleges and studied at universities in France, and they spoke French as well if not better than they did Arabic. They yearned for the French theater and French wit; they went to Paris every year and spoke of it as though it were home. They even gave their children French names—Pierre, Isabelle, Jacqueline— which must have sounded strange to foreign ears with such surnames as Nahas, Kheiralla, and Abdelnour.

One of our drivers, a Syrian, gave his son the modest name of Napoleon. Nowadays, Christians avoid giving their children European names, believing it will be a handicap if they intend to spend their lives in Egypt with its growing Arab nationalism.

French interest in the Levant dates as far back as the Crusaders, who are no doubt responsible for the many blue and green eyes amongst the Syrians and Lebanese. Some say it goes even further back than that to the time of Haroun-el-

Rashid, who is supposed to have signed a treaty with Charlemagne.

When the French Revolution broke out, France had held the leading place among the nations of the world for roughly a century and a half. Her language was the speech of civilized men everywhere; her literature, her arts and culture were proverbial; the splendor of Paris had been, if not seen, at least heard of far and wide. Paris was *la Reine du Monde*.

In both politics and trade, France was the leading European power in the Levant, but more important still, from the point of view of French influence there, was the fact that France, a Catholic state, considered herself the protector of the Christian minorities in the Moslem Ottoman Empire. As Ottoman influence waned in Egypt, French influence increased greatly. Although no treaty existed giving France any right as guardian of Christian interests, her role was automatically recognized by the other European powers.

The Greek Catholics, the Syrian Catholics, the Greek Orthodox, and the Maronites all looked to France as their champion, and what with her Jesuit schools and the devotion of her missionaries, France had practically no rivals.

Then the Suez baby was born, over whose guardianship powerful nations were to battle and Egypt herself was not to know a moment's peace. But at the time, it was a great triumph for French diplomacy. France owned some 50 per cent of the ordinary shares and most of the founder shares, and the Canal was managed entirely by a French staff. The Empress Eugénie herself came over especially for the celebrations for which the profligate Ismail was famous. Even more important, Ismail, because of the Canal, was himself in the hands of France. The Canal may have opened up a new route to the East, but it also opened up another highway leading to foreign intervention in Egypt's own house.

In archeology, too, France was in the lead in Egypt. It was a Frenchman, Champollion, who was the founder of Egyptology and who first deciphered the hieroglyphics, notably on the Rosetta Stone, which was unearthed by one of Napoleon's soldiers. Another Frenchman, Mariette, discovered the subterranean catacombs of the Apis bulls and was subsequently made conservator of Egyptian museums by Ismail. He was given the title of pasha. Later, Maspero accomplished some important work in Luxor and Karnak, and translated the inscriptions on the Pyramids at Sakkara. Important streets in Cairo are named after Champollion, Mariette Pasha, and Maspero.

During the First World War, Syria was taken from the Turks by the Allied Armies under General Allenby. After the War came the series of mandates. Great Britain withdrew in favor of France, and Syria and Lebanon became French mandated territories. Palestine, which under the Ottoman Empire had been an integral part of Syria, became a British mandate, while Egypt, of course, had been a British protectorate ever since the very outbreak of the War.

Strangely enough, in spite of the Protectorate, the British did not administer their own laws, and in the Mixed as well as the National Courts of Egypt, the legal system was modelled on the French Napoleonic Code.

The result of the Code was to increase French influence in Egypt greatly. Notwithstanding the British Occupation, Egypt looked to French judicial decisions and referred to French textbooks and French experts, and this no doubt is

49

one of the reasons why the social and cultural influence of France was so pronounced.

It wasn't really very surprising, therefore, that with parents and grandparents who had lived in a French sphere of influence in Syria, Lebanon, and Egypt, and been imbued with French culture, the first language we should learn to speak was French, and the first school we should go to was a French convent.

There, we too read French literature and were overpowered with the glories of French history. During the two years I spent at the convent school I never learned any other history or geography except that of France, but that in its minutest detail, down to the *Sous-Préfectures* and the wines of the different regions. We had one English lesson a week and we were taught no Arabic at all, in spite of the fact that we lived in Egypt. Father made Yvonne, Helen, and me take Arabic lessons at home.

Cramming and learning everything by heart, with long dreary periods of homework in the evening, seemed to be the French method of education in those days. It did not appear that we were required to think for ourselves at all. As long as we could recite Lamartine and whole chapters of *L'Histoire de France* by heart, regardless of whether we understood what we were talking about or not, we got good marks. Any deviation from the actual words quoted in the textbook was severely frowned upon.

Yvonne was blessed with a visual memory. All she had to do was look at a page twice and she could repeat it word for word, and spend the rest of the evening talking on the phone to Karim. But I'd labor for hours on my homework, trying to memorize the *grammaire,* the *Leçon des Choses,* and three chapters of *L'Histoire de France,* and the next day, I'd sit under the desk hoping Mother Mathilde would forget my existence and pick on anyone but me. But Mother Mathilde had apparently missed me since yesterday morning and longed to hear my voice. So I'd stand up and rattle off three lines and suddenly my memory would empty itself like a Tibetan monk's and I'd stop dead, and Yvonne would hiss the next two words to me and that would set me going at eighty miles an hour for the next six lines or so, and then I'd stop again. And so on.

If it hadn't been for my best friends, Sima and Rose, I would have been bottom of the class. As it was, *they* were. Not only were their memories like sieves, their French sounded exactly like their native Armenian. When they spoke of Lamartine, he was no longer the French poet, but Artine, the Armenian equivalent of Marius, from Erzeroum. The classical Armenian joke on Lamartine was that *Lam, il est parti, et Artine, il est resté.* If you think this isn't very funny, you've grasped the essence of the Armenian sense of humor.

Sima and Rose were identical twins, and what fascinated me about them was their hair. It stood straight up on end like live electrical wire, and I just couldn't take my eyes off it. The uniform—thick navy serge dresses, stiff white collars, floppy back cravats, and black shoes and stockings—had been designed to hide as much of us as possible, and, on looking back, in the case of Sima, Rose, and myself, this is by far the most sensible idea the convent school ever had.

I took to Sima and Rose like a fly to a sticky cake, and after a week at the convent, when I was even beginning to wear my hair like them, I went over and whispered—talking was strictly forbidden—my unbounded admiration. We have never let go of each other since. To this day, we are always telling one another that we haven't changed a bit since our schooldays, though why this should make us so happy, it is difficult to see.

Sima and Rose were boarders. This was undoubtedly very nice for their family, but it was harrowing for the convent, whose rules were very rigid where boarders were concerned. For instance, one rule laid down most emphatically that it was forbidden to look at yourself in the mirror, and Sima and Rose, for some reason best known to themselves, actually wanted to look at themselves in the mirror, especially when they fixed—so they thought—their hair in the morning.

As a deterrent, the mirror in the dormitory was covered with a sheet, which, incidentally, I found such a good idea that I did the same thing in my room at home. With their sensitive fingers, Sima and Rose would delicately remove the sheet, so delicately that the Dormitory Sister would come running before they had had time to pick up the mirror and start doing exotic things to their hair, and Sima and Rose would be reported to Mother Mathilde, who would in turn report them to the Mother Superior.

The strictest rule of all, however, concerned baths. Bath night was Saturday, and Saturday only, and the bath had to be taken while wearing a long-sleeved white nightdress, the emphasis being on clean minds rather than clean bodies. Foot-bath was on Thursday, and Thursday only, and the penalty for sneaking in an extra foot-bath was no foot-bath for two weeks, which in the warm weather was not only uncomfortable for the boarders but for everyone around.

Sima and Rose liked to indulge in baths as though bath-ing was the national Armenian pastime, and consequently they were always in disgrace. They never once received the *Grand Cordon d'Honneur* which was awarded once a month during an imposing ceremony worthy of Buckingham Palace, and at which the whole school gathered wearing white gloves. The good girls who did without baths, foot-baths, and looking at themselves in the mirror, and the others who could recite Lamartine without an Armenian accent and with the speed of a steam engine, would curtsy before the Mother Superior and rise again draped in a regalia which looked suspiciously like a curtain valance with tassels on it. It hung down to the feet and played around the ankles, with the result that half the time they were flat on their faces. But at least they had the satisfaction of knowing that they were Goodness personified.

One morning, Mother Mathilde, her voice trembling at the sinfulness she was about to expose, told how Sima, exasperated at having to wash herself under her nightgown, determined to find out if the other boarders really cleaned themselves in this weird manner. Having discarded her nightgown and rising like Venus from the waters, Sima peeped over the top of the partition to see how the girl in the next bath was making out.

The girl, a Greek by the name of Anastassoula, short for Anastasia, had also discarded her nightgown, but being real sharp and the pride of the convent school, had mistaken Sima for A MAN, and let off a series of long piercing blasts which had brought the Dormitory Sister running.

Sima, who was so sensitive she never even felt the flies glued to her, and once ate a cockroach which she found in her soup because she mistook it for a nice fat lentil from Upper Egypt, thought something was amiss, and tried to get into her soaking wet nightgown, but she couldn't manage it. By now, the rumor had got around the THE MAN had been seen in Sima's bath, and pandemonium reigned. The Dormitory Sister went around screaming, "Close your eyes, close your eyes, don't look at him," and the girls, trying to obey, with eyes closed and groping hands, ran right and left and into one another in their sopping-wet nightgowns.

Mother Mathilde paused in her racy account, her face, unlike Françoise Sagan's, crimson at having to relate such bathroom orgies. The whole class looked to the depraved Sima for an explanation—if explanation there could possibly be. But poor Sima was not only very uneloquent in every language except Armenian, she also had the pretty habit of talking of something feminine in the masculine and vice versa. All she could do was repeat over and over again in French, "*J'aime lui et moi prendre la bain ensemble sans la chemise,*" which may sound fine in Armenian but didn't help any in French.

Sima was put on a diet of soup and nice fat lentils from Upper Egypt for two weeks.

It had been a very exclusive school in more ways than one—so much so, in fact, that I have the decided feeling some of the exclusive things we indulged in were also exclusive to certain institutions. I am not only referring to the food, the midday meal invariably consisting of French fries—because, Rose was firmly convinced, it was a French school—and black olives—tiny little ones but with big stones —because, for all I know, this may be the perfect diet to "Look old and die young," or "Eat now, throw up later," or what have you.

The really exclusive thing I have in mind is sport. The Mother Superior, having decreed that tennis was not suitable for ladies in view of the shocking sight they would present in shorts, had decreed that we should go in for winter sports. If you think this isn't exclusive enough, then you've obviously not tried mountaineering in a basement on a clammy, khamseen day in Egypt, when the hot desert winds blow yellow dust even through the closed shutters, burning one's nose and throat.

The outfit, too, was ideal for the basement climate, and the thick black-and-white striped serge tunics with bloomers to match had the added advantage of making us look like inmates of a penitentiary. In this getup, even Sima and Rose had no desire to look at themselves in the mirror.

Tied to a long rope, we climbed cautiously from peak to peak, across mountains of glaciers and snow, on the lookout for crevasses and avalanches, while Mother Mathilde as the guide hollered such encouragement as, "We're nearly at the top of the Matterhorn," and, "You can put your foot down here, it's safe."

Bringing up the rear, to make quite sure that we didn't fall head-first into the abyss, was the "Angel," tottering under the weight of her *Grand Cordon d'Honneur,* which she had to wear at all times. "Angel" was the name given to certain senior girls because they were so good they weren't quite all there. And it is very sad to relate that this particular "Angel" not only hailed from Erzeroum but was also Sima and Rose's older sister.

For two years, until the French tide ran out and ushered

in the English, I attended the French convent school, reciting Lamartine and following the harrowing tales of Sima and Rose's lives as boarders. I cannot for the love of me understand why, after such an expensive and ladylike education, the only talent I seem to have is for belly-dancing.

5

Now It's à l'Anglaise

JUST AS I WAS BEGINNING TO SEE THE MATTERHORN ALL OVER the basement wall, and really beginning to get into the swing of things at the convent school, Mother suddenly whisked us out and put us into an English school which had just opened in a villa at Zizinia in Ramleh.

"That's all," she said. "French education is old-fashioned."

And that seemed to be that.

Sima and Rose, and most of our other friends, were whisked out as well, and we were all reunited on the British side.

It was 1936, the year the Anglo-Egyptian Treaty was signed.

I remember sitting in class and hearing the usual crowd of students and riffraff demonstrating and cheering outside the English Girls' College.

"Long Live Nahas Pasha," they screamed, "Long Live Nahas Pasha," for it was the squint-eyed Wafdist prime minister Nahas Pasha who had gone to London and negotiated the Treaty.

Of all Egyptian political figures in those days, Nahas Pasha was undoubtedly the most popular. The sight of the aging

57

Prime Minister strolling at Sidi-Bishr, his bulky shape in a black-and-white-striped bathing costume, and his eyes simultaneously facing East and West, was well known to all. Beside him walked Sousou, his plump, vivacious wife, considerably younger than he was, carrying a cream-colored parasol lined with green. More stories were told about Mustapha and Sousou el-Nahas than about the imaginary Arab character Goha.

Have you heard the one about Nahas Pasha at the big banquet, when he dug his fork into his neighbor's plate thinking it was his own? Or have you heard how Sousou called in the middle of the cabinet meeting because her bath water had been cut off? There was no end to the tales they told.

I remember Nahas Pasha arriving at Sidi-Gaber station soon after the signing of the Treaty. There were large crowds waiting for him as he stepped off the train followed by a retinue of portly officials in red fezzes. Along the platform he walked, while somebody carried the famous cream-colored parasol over his head. The crowds roared their welcome and the cheerleader yelled to his followers:

"Who is your father?"

To a man, the mobs cried back, "Nahas Pasha."

"Who is the father of the workers?" roared their leader.

"Nahas Pasha," roared back the crowd.

"Who do you all love?" cried the leader, who was now sitting on top of their heads.

"Nahas Pasha."

Nahas Pasha beamed. He was very pleased.

In spite of Egyptian nationalist aspirations and not-infrequent rioting, the British had been virtually occupying

Egypt since the bombardment of Alexandria in 1882, but with the Anglo-Egyptian Treaty, the British occupation was replaced by a twenty-year alliance.

Great Britain was permitted to station forces on Egyptian territory in time of peace as well as in time of war, "in view of the fact that the Suez Canal, while being an integral part of Egypt, is a universal means of communication between the different parts of the Empire." This was to be until such time as the Egyptian Army was in a position to insure the liberty and entire security of the Canal.

The British Forces were not to exceed ten thousand men and were to be stationed on either side of the Canal. Britain would defend Egypt if she was attacked and, in return, Egypt would give all the assistance in her power, such as the use of ports and airports.

The second point concerned the Sudan. The condominium by which Egypt and Great Britain had jointly administered the Sudan through the powers of a British Governor-General since the Sudan Convention of 1899 would continue until the Sudanese were ready for self-determination. The Egyptian and British Forces would then withdraw from the Sudan, thus enabling the Sudanese to determine their own future: either union with Egypt, or complete independence.

Lastly, Great Britain guaranteed Egypt's full sovereign rights. Egypt had never benefited from these because of the special privileges conferred upon European Christians as a result of treaties concluded between the Sultan of Turkey and most of the other important European countries, as well as the United States.

Powerful Great Britain, then in a position to impose her

will on others, was to use her influence with the other powers to get these special privileges or capitulations, as they were called, abolished.

Under the capitulations system, a foreigner held a most enviable position in Egypt, and was far better off than an Egyptian. The special privileges and immunities, however, led to many abuses. Not only were disputes between foreigners and Egyptians sometimes settled by diplomatic pressure, but it was difficult, for instance, to collect taxes on certain property belonging to foreigners and it was practically impossible to search the house of a foreigner, even if that foreigner was suspected of smuggling. Consequently, there was much smuggling among certain foreign communities. Foreigners were also tried in their own consular courts, or in the "mixed" courts.

But at the Conference of Montreux, which gathered all the interested parties the year following the Anglo-Egyptian Treaty, the capitulations were abolished. The "mixed" courts, however, were allowed to continue for a transition period of twelve years, after which the Egyptian National Courts would have sole judicial powers.

The Treaty appeared to go down well in Egypt, though it is difficult to say how much of the popular enthusiasm was whipped up by the Wafd party. Mobs are easily stirred and swayed in Egypt.

Great Britain had successfully managed to keep a foothold in Egypt and protect her strategic route to the East, and Egypt, having seen what happened to defenseless nations like Abyssinia, was for the moment not averse to allying herself with powerful Britain.

How long Egypt would remain satisfied with an agreement which enabled a foreign power to keep forces on her soil and virtually to occupy the Sudan as well was a matter for speculation, but it must have been obvious to many that Treaty obligations would not run as smoothly when the balance of power moved in Egypt's direction. For the moment, however, both parties seemed well pleased with themselves. "Treaty stamps" were issued in Egypt, and the anniversary of the signing of the Treaty was declared a public holiday.

The British were in. It was now fashionable to be heard speaking English, to collect a few English friends, and to give one's children the benefits of an English education.

There had long been an excellent English school for boys in Alexandria, founded at the turn of the century. The headmaster in the 1930's and until his death during the war had been Mr. Reed, a most capable and likable personality who had done much for Anglo-Egyptian friendship. But the first-class girls' schools, in spite of Italian propaganda and the huge Littorio School at Chatby, had been mainly French.

Now, with the opening of the English Girls' College, which was to be the largest English school for girls in the Middle East, an English education for girls definitely became the fashion. Parents withdrew their daughters from practically every school in Alexandria, for it was felt that narrow-mindedness and bigotry were no longer suited to the times, and that what was required was a more liberal education.

Perhaps the looks of the college itself, standing in the middle of vast playing fields, had something to do with its success, for it was a treat to the eyes, with its green rooftops and salmon pink walls. The architecture was in the Spanish-

61

American style. There was a patio with a fountain and pillars of blue mosaic, and parquet flooring throughout. There was a large turquoise swimming pool and a superb art room with windows all around it, while the domestic-science wing and beautifully equipped laboratories seemed to urge one to experiment. I wished I was five years old so that I could embark on my school days all over again in the brightly decorated kindergarten with the modern, pint-sized furniture, dollhouses, and paddling pool, instead of at the convent.

In the splendid dining room, the tables were round and friendly—no long refectory boards and hard benches here. Above all, one could talk, and talking to people and getting to understand them is what matters.

But when Mother's more conservative friends heard that Yvonne, Helen, and I had left the convent, they called up frantically to warn Mother that she would live to regret the day. "Chérie," they cried, "don't you know the English are mad? They allow girls far too much freedom. No, no, take it from us, there is no place like the convent." This last was certainly true.

Nevertheless, even those parents who thought it was fashionable to move with the times and give their daughters a British education were in for a few surprises where the new girls' college was concerned.

After the modest long sleeves and stockings of French convents in general, the summer uniform came as the first shock, for it consisted of not one, but half a dozen of the brightest colors I have ever seen in my life. Bare legs and open sandals not only were tolerated, but encouraged. I do not know who was responsible for the color scheme, but it may have had something to do with the headmistress, a charming and most unconventional Englishwoman.

At the tea party which she gave for the bewildered parents, she explained that she had in mind that the girls should all look like flowers.

"Daffodils and bluebells and marigolds," she said enthusiastically. "So gay, so gay, don't you think?" she added, addressing herself to Sima's and Rose's mother, who hadn't understood a word and was wondering, not without reason, how her daughters would look in duck-egg blue, venetian red, and the kind of yellow whch would suit dusters, but not her daughters.

Meanwhile, the fathers were finding it far less hard to go along with the English school system, for they were getting an eyeful of the good-looking young staff members who had just arrived from England, and they were in fact wishing that they could pick up a little something British themselves.

The Headmistress blew at a wisp of soft gray hair that had strayed onto her face, and went on to explain that each form would be known by the name of a poet. Any system graded by numbers would make it too much like school, "You do see that, don't you? Girls will be in Masefield and Longfellow." She smiled contentedly. "So refreshing, don't you think? And Byron and Tennyson. 'Tis better to have loved and lost . . . though actually, I don't know. You do remember that, don't you? And those girls who don't know any English can all go into Remove, and we'll have the names up on the door . . . " "Sima's name and Rose's . . . " began their mother, but the Headmistress went rambling on about a host of golden daffodils, and with a Hey and a Ho and a Hey Nonny No.

Mothers looked at one another in consternation. Perhaps their friends had been right and they should have left their daughters at the convent schools to be brought up in the good old-fashioned way. After all, this was the East. First it had been the uniforms, and now the poets. What was this Lamb, apart from what you ate on Sham-el-Nessim? Tennyson they had vaguely heard of, but who was "Remove"?

"Please Meeess," one Syrian mother ventured to ask the Headmistress, "I don't understand what classes my daughters Naila and Adèle they go into."

"Now, let me see," said our headmistress, looking it up in her if-it's-madness-it's-British manual. "Oh yes, here it is." She made an effort to speak very slowly, as though she were talking to a cretin.

"Naila is in Chau-cer, and Adèle is in Shake-speare."

Turning round to her friend, the baffled mother drawled in her Syrian-Arabic, "Darling, on your life, tell me, what did she say?"

"On my life, Darling," replied the friend, also in a drawling Syrian-Arabic, "I didn't understand what she said about Naile, but Adèle is taking lessons with a sheik. It's not right for an English school. But between you and me, the English are mad."

For months, the bewildered mothers, pioneers of the British experiment, worked themselves into a liver condition throwing coffee party after coffee party to discuss the latest innovations of the school, and argued themselves hoarse as to which was the higher, Milton, Byron, or Stevenson.

But we had never enjoyed school so much. With the Headmistress and her young staff exhorting us to fresh air, exercise, and fair play, we spent most of the time rushing around the playing fields, wielding hockey sticks, lacrosse sticks, and cricket bats, and making floral designs in the beautiful swimming pool. We were always in need of a new pair of shorts or a tennis racket, and the only sport we did not go in for was mountaineering.

Lessons were not the usual run of the mill either, and the Syrian mother whose daughter Adèle was in Shakespeare was able to report that all the members of the class had been urged to produce photographs of themselves as infants, which had been exhibited in the art room. The idea was to guess who was who, which, according to the Headmistress, was excellent training—for what, the Syrian mother wasn't quite sure, but it was in lieu of the history lesson.

Mother, too, was very upset at having to communicate the result of a debate involving Milton and Masefield and a couple of other poets. The item discussed had had something to do with who benefited mankind most, Pasteur or Mickey Mouse, and Mickey Mouse had won hands down.

What captivated our imaginations, however, was the stage, which was very professional. By the time we were due to leave school every single one of us quite convinced she was an undiscovered Ingrid Bergman. One term, with such talent as Sima and Rose, and in keeping with the tradition of the school to do things off the beaten track, we decided to put on a variety show. It was not quite of the Ziegfeld type, but it was called "Follies," which, everyone agreed after-wards, described it perfectly, and when all of Alexandria had seen it, half the communities in town refused to speak to us.

Sima and Rose insisted on doing a number they had

65

written themselves—the script consisted of four words—because they said it would be a sure hit, and it was rather unfortunate that we let them, because their number did hit quite a few people in the face. Wearing a wild look which belonged to her, and a leopard skin which belonged to her brother—he was called Brj—Sima swung from a rope high above the stage and landed on top of the heads of the select Alexandria audience who thought they had come to see one of the classics.

With her hair fixed in such a way that she could hardly see where she was going, she ran up and down the rows of screaming bejewelled women, jabbering excitedly, "Me Tarzan, me Tarzan." Meanwhile, Rose, left behind on the stage and similarly attired except that her leopard skin came from the floor of an Armenian doctor's surgery, uttered heart-rending cries of "Me Jane."

The *pièce de résistance* was a skit on the Lebanese written by Yvonne, who was very clever at whipping up sketches, and played by three Lebanese girls including herself. Although they followed the script closely at first, they soon went berserk and you couldn't tell the difference between them and Cousin Elise, who has a heart of gold and a bank account to match; and the broker's wife, who, before you have finished ringing her doorbell, rams her homemade baklava down your throat; and our friend Adèle's aunt, whose only conversation is food, and who, when asked how she liked Paris, answered that you could have it, because the French couldn't cook potatoes as well as they cooked them in Beiteddin.

The audience was in stitches. The Armenians laughed themselves silly, little imagining what Sima and Rose had in store for them later on in the program, and the Lebanese, too, screeched delightedly, bless them, until they realized we were imitating them.

After the show, Aunt Elise, who had been sitting in the second row and who had unwittingly been Yvonne's source of inspiration, came up to her and said, "Chérie, on your life, tell me and I won't tell a soul. Who could you possibly have been imitating? Do I know her?"

But the English system caught on, and we were all very proud of the school, Moslem, Christian, and Jew alike. The girls were of every race and religion and, though at times the place sounded like the Tower of Babel, we got on very well together. We even had our own smoothly-running parliament and elected our own prefects and head-girl. Though at first many of the pupils could not speak a word of English, when they left it was difficult to believe that the majority of them had never been to England and did not speak English at home. The ones who spoke the most impeccable English were the Copts. It seemed strange to see these usually very dark girls switch from faultless Arabic to faultless English without any apparent effort at all.

People who say that the English are mad are those who do not understand them, but I think that having spent half my life with English governesses, having been educated at an English school, and having lived in England for a number of years, I am fairly well qualified to say most emphatically that the English are not mad. No, sir. *Insane.* Or, as Adèle's aunt used to say, "The British are all right, but they are not like the Lebanese." She seemed to think it was a pity.

I can look back on my English education with real pride at the many accomplishments which I am still hoping will come in handy one day soon. They haven't yet, of course, but the list of talents is nonetheless very impressive.

I can play hockey and lacrosse and left-handed cricket when some lucky people don't even know the meaning of these words. I can climb ropes when there are perfectly good stairs, and I can vault a horse and slip a disc. I can walk into any cocktail party looking as though I am swinging a cricket bat and don't know where to park my half-dozen arms and legs, and I can do somersaults, classical Greek flying leaps, and even the splits, all after one Martini. I can shove peas on the back of my fork and drop them all over the floor, and after years of special elocution lessons, I can say, "Um, ah," for hours on end and still sound Lebanese. I know that I must be a good sport because that's what the British call a rotten tennis player, and I can cook food *à l'Anglaise*. The only trouble is that no one will ever eat it.

Being Eligible—The Marriage Market

IN THE BACKWARD AREAS LIKE EUROPE AND THE UNITED States, where they don't understand the first thing about women—or the Middle East or anything else—when a girl finishes school or college she looks around for a job, starts agitating for equal pay with men, and then proceeds to make a thorough nuisance of herself.

But in the East, where Men are Men and not Mice, and they know how to treat women, men don't stand for this sort of nonsense. As a matter of fact, they don't often stand up for a lady at all. It's the lady who stands up for the man— if she knows what is good for her, that is. The only man who would make a woman walk in front of him would be walking in a mine field.

Every Oriental, even if he is an idiot, knows instinctively what a woman should and should not do, and she should not do anything except wait on him, so he does not have to bother about asking her advice. He knows that Western women are too free and that freedom for women is bad for men—very bad indeed. The only career a woman should have is looking after her husband, and sometimes, if she's lucky, he may call in up to three more women to help her do this, so that she won't get tired.

Instead of going down on bended knees and being grateful that we were in the East, where they are so considerate towards women, Sima, Rose, and I had visions of ourselves launching out into the world on our own feet and having careers.

Mirage. It was all the fault of the British. With our heads pumped full of English-school nonsense about women getting jobs, we had overlooked the fact that we had a Special Mission in Life. One that was the most hazardous, most exciting of all callings. It was known as Being Eligible, and what you had to do was sit back with some nice bit of embroidery and catch a husband.

After a varying amount of sewing, the good obedient girls who did as their parents bade them were rewarded by finding husbands who provided large houses, children, and security. Some of these girls were very happy, especially if in time of a man shortage they had caught somebody else's husband.

Others were whisked out of school before the end of term, and before they had even started on their embroidery, to marry someone they hadn't so much as set eyes on. Perhaps it was just as well. Anyway, they had the whole of their lives to get a good look at him. Sometimes, the bridegroom was a little older than the bride—twenty-odd years or so. Sometimes, instead of twice her age, he was twice her size, and sometimes, unfortunately, he was both. Perhaps the prospective bridegroom owed a man some money and that man just happened to have six daughters, or perhaps he had just walked into a trap. No matter. The daughters knew that their parents had far more experience than they did in such matters, and anyway, they were always delighted at missing end-of-term exams. The bridegrooms too were delighted to

70

have nice young brides and fat dowries, and so everyone was happy.

When the good obedient girls had caught husbands, they liked to look around pityingly at those other girls who had been sewing for half a decade and whose house was so full of petit point they had to give it away like coffee in Brazil.

Sima, Rose, and I and two other friends—Beatrice, who devoured books on Freedom, and Adèle, whose parents thought her rather simple because she wasn't content with wearing beautiful clothes but also wanted to design them—were the despair of our families.

Sima and Rose wanted to be interpreters, I wanted to go on the stage, and all Beatrice wanted to do was be able to take the tram unchaperoned. When I told Mother and Father of my ambition, they greeted it much as though I had announced the intention of being lavatory attendant at Piccadilly Circus. Sima and Rose fared no better. In fact, their mother was so upset she couldn't speak anything but Armenian for a whole week. Our families had not got together to put forward the same arguments as to why we should not do anything, but it all went under the logical heading of "It isn't done." As to what we should do with our diplomas, the idea was that we should put them away in a drawer and only bring them out to regale our husbands of a dull rainy evening.

We had reached the point where the old way of life had met up with the new, and we were caught unable to move forward or back. It would have been far better if we had remained at the convent school, or never even gone to school at all, or indeed, never learned to read or write. Then we might have been able to slop contentedly around the house, with brocade dressing gowns on our backs, some embroidery in our hands, and nothing in our heads. Under those conditions, the transition from being first under the authority of one's family to being under the domination of a husband would have been quite painless and natural.

The five of us usually spent the day at Sidi-Bishr Beach bemoaning our fate. Chaperoned by a governess apiece, we'd sit on the sand watching the horizon, talking of all the things we would have liked to do and couldn't.

"Across there lies America, where women are the men," Sima, would say, blissfully ignorant that she was staring straight at Cyprus.

Then, after we had eaten four sticky cakes each and Adèle had remarked that at this rate we'd soon look like some of our bulging relatives, we'd go to the Sporting Club and play tennis.

But we had a friend who was far worse off than we were. She was an Egyptian girl by the name of Soraya with whom we had made friends at the convent school. Her family was very worried about her, for Soraya was getting to be an old maid. Like us, she was nineteen and unmarried, and it was all her own fault, too.

Even if she didn't like petit point she wouldn't have had to sew for long, for she was most generously endowed by nature both with looks and feddans of land in Upper Egypt. Every day of the week, Fridays and Sundays included, suitors lined up three deep at her father's door to ask her hand in marriage, but Soraya would have nothing to do with them. Nothing. She wouldn't so much as look at the candidates. Not even a glimpse at the one who had six hundred water buffalo. Somewhere, somehow, the clueless girl had heard that people married for love.

At regular intervals, her father showed her half a dozen little squares which he had drawn on a sheet of paper. In each square was the name of a suitor and the few important details about him which were of interest—not whether he had one eye, for instance, but whether he had one million.

Soraya lived in dread of marrying one of "the little squares."

"Choose anyone you like," her father would say generously.

What more could a girl want? But the silly Soraya refused to consider any of them. Her poor father was at a loss to understand where his daughter had developed such an unpleasing personality, for she had been most properly brought up both at home and at the convent school, and had never so much as been allowed even to cross the street unchaperoned.

One afternoon, Sima, Rose, and I decided to go round to Soraya's house and find out how many buffalos the latest suitor had.

We went down to our garage. Raimondo, our new chauffeur—our turnover of chauffeurs was as impressive as our turnover of governesses—was sitting by the car, thumbing his way through a movie magazine. He was a good-looking Italian who not only drove fast but *was* fast. He'd leer at Yvonne, who was going through a book-reading phase, and he'd tell her that there were other things in life besides books, Signorina, which he'd like to tell her about. One day, Yvonne absent-mindedly asked "What?" and Raimondo told her. Yvonne was so shaken she didn't dare tell Mother till months later.

"To Mademoiselle Soraya's, please, Raimondo."

"Si, Signorina. La Signorina Yvonne, she no coming?"

"*Non,* she no coming."

Soraya's house was near Mustapha Barracks. Soraya's father very prudently always kept the shutters tightly closed so that she wouldn't be tempted to look out the window at the British Army in all shades of regimental dress and undress.

One day, an enterprising lieutenant who had been very impressed with the brief glimpse he had caught of Soraya, had sent an enormous bunch of red roses with his orderly and then rolled up optimistically at Soraya's front door, but although he had spent a couple of hours in the house and drunk six cups of Turkish coffee, Soraya had never been allowed to appear.

We rang the bell and asked if Soraya was in. The suffragi said yes, and showed us into the living room, the shutters of which were, as usual, tightly closed. The room was cluttered with ugly ornaments and pictures of relatives all over the walls, and the little coffee tables were in the Oriental style, inlaid with mother-of-pearl. Chairs and sofas were covered with white dust sheets. Many people did this during the summer to make the house look cooler and protect all the petit point and furniture from dust and moths. I hated this habit. It seemed senseless to protect furniture which would live longer than we would anyway.

Sima, Rose, and I waited for what seemed like a long time. The suffragi reappeared with three little purple-and-gold cups of Turkish coffee and three glasses of water. What on earth could be keeping Soraya?

We were beginning to wonder whether we shouldn't perhaps leave, when her father came in fingering his amber beads. I have never seen him without them.

He was a big, flabby man, sallow and completely bald, with a generous paunch and three chins. He always wore dark glasses, even inside the house. He asked us if we'd had coffee, and when we said "yes," he called the suffragi and ordered him to bring coffee.

We chatted for a while.

"How is your father?" he asked me.

"He's very well, thank you."

"Allah be praised," he replied. "And your mother?"

"She's very well, too, thank you," I said.

"Allah be praised," he said again. "And your sister?"

"Which one?"

"The pretty one," he said.

"She's very well, thank you."

"Allah be praised," he said, twiddling the beads. "When is she getting married?"

"Well, she's not really engaged yet," I answered. "She's only eighteen."

"That's just the right age. Tell your father to marry her off before the young man changes his mind. I hear he is a very nice young man, very rich."

"Yes, he's very nice. Please, er . . . is Soraya not in?" I finally ventured to ask.

"I've locked her up in her room," he replied, twiddling his beads nervously. "Again today, I offered her a choice of five eligible men, all of them from good, highly respected

75

families. She could pick any one she liked. A choice of five, I tell you. When I married I had no choice at all. Aren't I a good father? Aren't I being reasonable? You know, she wouldn't even look at my list. She's nineteen, she's not young any more. It's high time she was married and had children. I'm a patient man, but patience has its limits. So I've locked her in her room until she comes to her senses."

We drank our coffee and left feeling very sorry for Soraya.

"I wonder what she is going to do," said Rose. "She can't say no forever."

When I called Soraya's place the next day, I was told that instead of coming to her senses, Soraya had come out through the window and, in bedroom slippers, had gone and married a handsome young lawyer she had met at the riding school.

As it turned out, the marriage did not work, which all goes to show that parents know best and that girls should be kept in their places.

Part of the curriculum of Being Eligible consisted of being shown off like prize cattle at all the balls, cocktail parties, and cinema premières with which Alexandria was rife. Each community in town had clubs and organizations to help support its less fortunate members. There wasn't a day when the ladies of some community didn't swoop down on the various offices, banks, and stores to sell tickets for benefit balls in aid of their respective societies.

Sometimes, the clever ones managed to throw in a couple of words to advertise their husbands' business or their Eligible Daughters.

"My daughter made this petit point bag herself," the clever one would say—she'd probably bought it at some charity bazaar. "Yes, it is pretty, isn't it? She cooks, too. My daughter, of course. Ah, these modern girls who don't know a thing about how to keep house. You should taste her little cheese tarts. My daughter's, of course. They melt in your mouth. The tarts. It so happens I've got some with me"—she had just bought them at Baudrot's. "I was going to take them to my sister's. You know my daughter goes to the Catholic Foyer twice a week, where they teach them lots and lots of excellent things. She is not like this new generation which is only fit for the cabarets. Yes, lots and lots of things . . . er, er . . . er . . . how to keep a good Christian home, look after children, you know, and . . . and . . . and . . . lots and lots of things. What a lovely figure my daughter has, too. You should see it. She follows the exercises on the radio every morning, you know."

Then the other lady would start, for two ladies always went together to demoralize whoever it was they were selling tickets to.

"Now," she'd say with a filthy look, "I know you won't refuse five tickets for the Fallen Women's Fund."

Since the businessman's business on the side had no doubt contributed to the downfall of a couple of them, there wasn't much he could do but agree to contribute to their salvation. Anyway, his wife would be sure to get her own back when it was her turn to sell tickets for the Armenian comedy which to everyone except an Armenian would turn out to be a first-class tragedy.

It was our duty—Yvonne and I, Sima, Rose, Adèle, and the other Eligibles—to make the rounds of all the balls in Alexandria. If it wasn't A Night in Athens, with *Boozoukia* songs and *retzina* wine—which incidentally, tastes exactly like turpentine—it was a Red Crescent Carnival in aid of

77

the Children of Upper Egypt, or an Evening at the Swiss Club, where you could see the good ladies of the Swiss colony, dressed in their national costumes, raking in the foreign money as usual, and prancing around like two-ton Valkyries. Or perhaps it was a Syrian Catholic Ball, or a Syrian Maronite Ball (there's a difference), or a Syrian Orthodox Ball, or even a ball in aid of the little White Russians. I only knew of three White Russian families in Alexandria, but on the night of the ball, everybody's name seemed to end with "off"—even the Greek grocer's. And everyone poured the vodka down and reminisced about St. Petersburg. I don't know whether they had ever been outside Egypt, but after a few vodkas nobody cared, and anyway, it was a particularly good ball.

Alexandria was especially famous for its "little" cocktail parties, thrown for no reason at all except to see and be seen and get one's picture in the Sunday papers. If there was a reason, it was probably a good one, like a farewell party in honor of somebody who was meant to be leaving next week and would still be here in ten years' time, because having lived in Alexandria, one couldn't bear to live anyplace else. But no matter what kind of party, it was always referred to as "little," for everything Alexandrians did was on a little scale—the Louis XIV kind.

The invitation sometimes came in the form of a printed card, but more often than not, the phone would ring and a Friend of Mother's would screech, "Chérie, I'm giving a little cocktail party on Thursday. No, Chérie, a very little party. Just a few of my very close friends, you know."

Mother knew. She did the same. "Very close" meant very close to two hundred. The Friend continued, "What? You can't come? I won't hear of it. You, my best friend! You simply must come, and your husband and your dear daughters, too. And who are they imitating this time, ha, ha, ha. Well, it's settled then. There'll be nobody at all, Chérie. Really. There'll be just ourselves."

So Mother would find herself saddled with her third cocktail party on Thursday, plus the happy prospect of breaking the glad tidings to Father, who detested cocktail parties and had even been known to fall asleep at one.

Helen was too young for cocktail parties, but Yvonne and I were expected to accompany Mother and Father and be seen everywhere. Yvonne loved balls, cocktail parties, and social gatherings of all kinds. In the midst of the well-dressed women, the expensive perfume, the small talk, and the smoky atmosphere, she was like a native in the jungle. But not I. I seemed to grow eight arms and legs; I tripped over all the furniture; my eyes watered and my feet ached. I would have been far happier in the kitchen.

Yvonne had Karim to fuss around her at parties. Although it was a foregone conclusion that they would eventually marry—in fact they had the blessing of both families—Yvonne was not allowed to go out alone with him even to a movie. Karim approved of this, for it meant that Yvonne didn't go out with other men either, and so she only saw him at parties and family gatherings.

Sima, Rose and I hated these parties and the very sound of the words "Eligible Men," who, if truth were told, hated nothing so much as the company of nice "Eligible Girls." Whenever they saw one come in through the door, they promptly fled through the window and made for the third-rate cabarets downtown.

Consequently, our substitutes for Karim and Prince Charming were a couple of Armenian photographers who came to take pictures of the guests and who invariably insisted on photographing us from the rear because they said it was more flattering, and the father of one of our schoolfriends, a harmless little man if one could have tied his hands and put him behind bars. He had a lisp and a terrific aptitude for pinching his daughter's friends.

On the way in the car, Mother would say to me, "Please smile dear, you have quite nice teeth. I just don't know why it is that clothes seem to do so little for you."

She wasn't the only one who didn't know. Neither did plump Mademoiselle Stefanakis, the "little" Greek dressmaker who was always out of breath and came to fit us at home. With Yvonne, all she had to do was carelessly drape the material—any old bit of material—around her, and Yvonne was a resplendent vision. With me, no matter what she did, I was a sight. Desperate, Mademoiselle Stefanakis would crawl on all fours, getting more and more out of breath, shoving pins into her mouth with the insatiable appetite of a fire-eater. She'd snip little bits off here and there, then wish she hadn't and try and pin them back. Then she'd look at me and dispense some Greek logic to the effect that it takes all kinds to make a world. Mother would be called in for consultation and after she and Mademoiselle Stefanakis had shaken their heads and said "tsk, tsk, tsk" at least forty times, Maha would bring them some coffee and it would be unanimously voted that it wasn't the dress which did nothing for me, but me who did nothing for the dress.

We never arrived at a party on time, but always an hour late—even if we had to drive round the block for ten minutes. We were embarrassingly over-punctual in the family, but if one turned up at a party on time one was more than likely to find the hostess in her bath. The later one arrived, the smarter one was.

The street would be lined with insignificant little Cadillacs, but no camels. Those were exclusive to the American tourists. Chauffeurs would be standing in little groups talking and smoking. We knew them all, for at some time or other they had all been with us. There'd be Piero, who was always so impatient to get going that he invariably slammed the door on Father's rear end, nearly propelling him out the other side; Habib, which in Arabic means "beloved," but he wasn't because he smelled of garlic; and the old Sudanese with gray hair and glasses who was the first to admit that he hadn't driven anything but a horse before, though he always added enthusiastically that he loved cars.

We said good evening to them, remembering the many times they had driven us frantic, and walked towards the little villa with the cheery little lights of a thousand watts each. The little sandy path was like every sandy path, lined with quite ordinary pots of tulips, the bulbs of which had come from Holland, and little colored lights were hidden inside them.

The front door was flung open before we had had time to ring by a little suffragi six feet tall, with very black skin and two large scars on his face to denote his tribe. He wore a red and gold livery, but it wasn't real gold, so nobody was impressed. It was his specific duty to stand behind the door on the lookout for the guests.

The hub of conversation hit us in the face. The house was full of people. Close to two hundred was about right.

"Chérie," cried the Typical Alexandria Hostess, throwing her arms wide and embracing Mother with little kissing noises in the air.

"Chérie, how are you, I haven't seen you in ages," cried Mother and the Hostess both at the same time and without waiting for an answer.

Father stood by patiently. He was used to this kind of scintillating conversation. He knew that "ages" was last night at a precisely similar party.

"Chérie," continued Mother at the top of her voice, "let me look at you." Mother was very good at memorizing other women's gowns. "You look ravishing, Chérie."

The Hostess wore a plain black dress, so plain it obviously came straight from Paris.

"Chéries," she cried to Yvonne and me, "the young people are over by the buffet."

As we moved off, we could hear the Hostess cry to the latest arrivals, this time in perfect English instead of French:

"Darling, how are you? How nice of you to come to my little party. I haven't seen you in ages." She was like those dolls one winds up. She had done it so often, it came quite naturally and she appeared to be really enchanted to see everybody.

There would be a picture in the Sunday paper with the caption: "The divine hostess in a Balmain creation is seen greeting her distinguished guests."

We were swallowed in the crowd of beautifully gowned women and prosperous balding men—the less hair, the more money—and suffragis in elaborate red and gold outfits passing round trays of drinks and hors-d'oeuvres. Rings caught the light on well-manicured hands and trails of cigarette smoke were beginning to collect round the crystal chandeliers. Everyone seemed to be screaming, "Chérie, how are you, I haven't seen you in ages." The crowd was the usual melting pot of Levantines and Europeans—Syrian, Maltese, Armenian, Italian, French. There were Britishers who had married handsome women from Smyrna, wealthy Greeks from Khartoum, Egyptians with British, American, or German wives, beautiful Turkish princesses, Copts who had married their own cousins. I knew most of the people by sight—the Governor of Alexandria, the Governor of the Municipality, the British Chief of the Alexandria Police, and the Turkish Consul, whose daughter Zeinap was at the English Girls' College with me.

I liked the name Zeinap. She was a green-eyed beauty with long black lashes and thick black hair and freckles. She spoke five languages fluently—with an American accent, since they had lived in the States—and she looked exactly like her mother, except that her mother spoke only Turkish.

"I hate parties, too, though it is very undiplomatic of me to say so," whispered her father in my ear. I liked him. "Zeinap is at the buffet table with all the young people."

I threaded my way through the vast, lavishly furnished salons with the high ceilings and big windows framed with heavy velvet curtains. What if I should meet my Prince Charming between 7 and 9 P.M.? Paintings and Aubussons adorned the walls and there were valuable bibelots enclosed in glass cases. Would he look like Fleeting Chin talking big over there? After all, as Robert's mother the Pekinese was fond of saying, a man doesn't have to be beautiful unless he is penniless. Fleeting Chin probably had a lot of character, most of it in the form of shares.

83

Large silver cigarette boxes could be seen on every available table-top, and Persian rugs with soft muted shades and delicate patterns covered most of the highly polished parquet floors. Or maybe I might even wreck a happy home between 7 and 9 P.M. Wouldn't everyone be surprised? Me the first! Vases of cut glass and baskets of gladioli were everywhere. It wasn't my idea of home sweet home, though so many homes were like this one in Alexandria, but the house undeniably had intrinsic beauty. Or maybe I could . . .

"Jacqueline, Chérie," a voice cried. Startled, I tripped over the rug and found myself at the foot of the Pekinese. She was wearing a mink coat and her hair was dyed a bright mauve. Next to her on the pale gray satin sofa sat a dowager the spitting image of a bulldog—but one could see that she must have been beautiful in her youth. It was strange how people could look like animals.

It reminded me of when I was five and Mother had sent for me to meet some of her guests. I had curtsied all the way round, and then Mother had said, "You forgot to say good evening to the gentleman over there," and I had replied in my best party manners, "Where, *Maman?* Oh. *Excusez-moi,* Monsieur, I thought you were a monkey."

"Don't you recognize me?" asked the Bulldog. "I was at school with your Grandmother."

Poor Granny, I thought.

"Really?" I said, and giggled hideously. The English Girls' College would have been proud of me.

"How old are you, Chérie?" inquired the Pekinese.

"Nineteen."

"Nineteen already? How time flies," she mused. "Tsk, tsk,

84

tsk, it's time you were married and had children. What wouldn't a girl give for a nice husband like Robert!"

I can't think of a thing, I thought.

"All the girls are crazy about Robert," the Pekinese went on.

Maybe they're crazy, I thought.

"Really?" I said.

"Wouldn't you like a nice husband? Like Robert, say?" she asked.

No, I thought.

"I'm too young to think of husbands," I said, and giggled like one demented.

"No, you're not," said the Pekinese, shaking a plump finger with a massive ring on it. "I was married at sixteen and my husband died four years later."

It figures, I thought.

"I'm sorry," I said.

"Quick, Chérie," said the Bulldog, her jowls quivering, her bulging eyes about to fall out of their orbits, "who is the girl misbehaving with the British officer?"

It's a Greek friend of mine named Sophie, I thought.

"I don't know," I said.

"She is behaving outrageously," said the Pekinese, devouring her through her lorgnette. "Can you hear what they are saying, Chérie?"

I turned round. Sophie was sitting on a chair and the officer stood beside her, talking about banalities. The only thing they seemed to be indulging in was a cigarette.

"Do you know," whispered the Bulldog excitedly, "I saw them crossing the street together this morning, rue Fouad it was, just by Pastroudis and the Rio Cinema. It was ex-

85

actly a quarter to twelve. Really, I daren't think where they were coming from."

"Pastroudis perh——" I began.

"Really, Jacqueline, don't be naive," said the Pekinese.

"Oh!" I said, and blushed.

"Really, what is this generation coming to," said the Bulldog.

"So loose, so immoral. Tsk, tsk, tsk, what next? It shouldn't be allowed. I wonder if they are engaged?"

If a girl was seen out once with a man, let alone a man in a British uniform, she was engaged. If she was seen out with him twice, her reputation was in shreds. Neither Sima, Rose, Adèle, Yvonne, nor I were allowed out alone with men, no matter how eligible, but we would not be such fools as to cross the main street of Alexandria for everyone to see us.

"Go along and have fun with the young people," said the Pekinese generously, dismissing me. She leaned forward, took a cigarette from the silver box on the low table before her, and a suffragi appeared like a genie to light it for her. Then she and her bosom friend the Bulldog continued to stare at everybody and whisper loudly, "Did you see so-and-so," or "Look at so-and-so."

The sliding doors giving onto the dining room were wide open and the buffet stretched the whole length of the vast room. It was piled high with food laid out on silver dishes, and only the sides of the heavy lace cloth were visible. Although it was only a cocktail party, there would be dinner later on. At about eleven, the fleet of suffragis would swiftly remove what was there and bring on the turkeys with brown rice and raisins, the rolled vine leaves, the stuffed pigeons and the quails, the enormous fish, and a multitude of desserts. After all the guests had eaten off specially laid little tables brought out like magic from the depths of the house, the buffet would still look untouched, and all the food would go to the cooks and suffragis, as well as to the chauffeurs and parking attendants, and Ahmed the beggar, who patronized every party in town and who, many said, owned a block of flats. "Let them eat cake."

There they were, the young people, among them my friends, Sima and Rose and Adèle, standing awkwardly, looking for all the world like the personification of a good English-school upbringing which teaches you everything except what to do with your hands and feet. Yvonne and Zeinap were different. No need for them to read up on "How to look fetching," for they could fetch them anytime. That's what came of being born with charm.

Once when Adèle and I had been arguing as to whether a friend of ours was pretty or not, Adèle had said, "If you really want to know, just watch the men."

I was watching the men right now. They were all standing on their heads, trying to outdo one another for Yvonne and Zeinap, who were laughing like a couple of goats and, for intelligent girls, making some very asinine remarks.

Adèle had also said that Men did not like intelligent girls, which, she explained, accounted for our lack of success with the opposite sex. "We're too clever," she said modestly, "that's what." It seemed that the more stupid women were, the better. "Look around you at all the brilliant men who have married nitwits," Adèle had remarked. It made men feel good, apparently, and Yvonne and Zeinap were obviously dumb enough to make the men feel good. If that's all there was to being a success, it was simple.

"Hullo," said Robert the Eligible. He wasn't really bad-looking when you thought of a moose, and there was no other man around except Gamal, our suffragi who had been borrowed by the hostess for the evening.

"Oh . . . oh . . . hullo Robert."

"Yvonne is looking very lovely tonight," he said.

"Yes, we have the same dressmaker."

"Really?" he said, "I would never have thought it."

"Would you care for some cotton?" Robert asked, holding out a plateful of canapés. "That white stuff looks just like cotton, don't you think?"

"Er . . . er . . . no, thank you."

"Cotton is a wonderful thing," he said, in the same tones a Frenchman would use if he were talking of his mistress. "I don't know what the world would do without cotton."

"Oh I don't either, Robert," I gushed. "Robert, what *would* it do without cotton?"

"I just don't know, Jacqueline. It's a terrible thought."

"Terrible." I was ready to cry.

"I didn't know you were so interested in cotton, Jacqueline."

"I didn't either, Robert, but after all, where would we be without cotton? I mean, mattresses stuffed with cotton, pillows . . . and . . . and . . . how would I be able to clean my ears without cotton?"

"If only we could find a way to strike a death blow to that murderous cotton worm. If we don't do something about it, it'll eat all the cotton and that'll be the end of us. And you know where we'd be without cotton."

"Oh, Robert, I daren't think."

"Mother's right," said Robert. "She's been talking to me quite seriously about you."

"What did she say?"

"Quick, look over there," he said, grabbing hold of my arm. "That dress there looks like satin, but I'll bet it's cotton. They can do anything with cotton nowadays. Anything."

"Oh! Can they really, Robert?"

Two elegant women in tight-fitting dresses came over to the buffet. They looked like panthers, sleek and smooth with large mascaraed eyes, but by the time they reached thirty-five, if they continued to indulge in soft living, they would be fat and flabby, and at sixty, they would probably look like the Bulldog, but their friends would say, "You should have seen them when they were young—the most beautiful women in town."

They stood for a moment looking at the table groaning under the mass of food. So fattening, all that food. They inspected the centerpiece of roses and narcissus, the ecru table cloth, the lace doilies, the tempting hors-d'oeuvres from Baudrot's, the delicious homemade specialities. They would have to have a massage again tomorrow. One put on weight just looking. Then, daintily, with their beautiful long white hands which had never known any rough manual work in their lives, they picked black olives, looked at them again, and popped them into their beautifully painted mouths.

"Chérie, I hope you'll be able to come to the première at the Royal Cinema on Friday," said one of the Panthers. "It should be very good. I forgot what it's called and I don't know who is acting in it, but everybody will be there. The Governor, the Diplomatic Corps, everybody, everybody.

Wait, Chérie, I do remember what it was called. It was called 'Coming Short-lee' or 'Short-lee Coming,' but my English is not very good."

"Chérie," cried the other Panther, "it sounds like an excellent film. Oh, have you seen what Clea is wearing? Over there. That neckline. She says it's Paris but I say it's indecent. Oh dear, here she comes. Clea, Chérie, you look ravishing. What a lovely dress. I just love the neckline. Do turn round and let me look at you. Isn't she sensational, Chérie? Unforgettable, you can tell it's Paris. And tell me, Chérie, how are you, I haven't seen you in ages."

In French pervaded with a Greek accent, Clea replied that "eh, Chérie," she was as well as could be, "eh," since with all this talk of war, "Chérie, eh," what do you expect, she hadn't been able, "eh, Chérie," to take her annual cure at Vichy, "eh." These were rough times. One had to care for one's liver when one lived in hot countries, Chérie.

"Do you really like my little dress, Chérie," she continued, "take it, it's yours. There's really nothing to it. Chérie, do look over there. Charles with his latest. Really, at his age. He never changes, does he, only wives that is, ha, ha, ha." "They say she's French," said one of the Panthers. "Really, Chérie," said Clea, "and from which sidewalk, eh?"

As we were getting ready to go, I remember seeing a British couple who had just arrived in Alexandria take leave of their hosts. They were terribly stiff and terribly British. And they were also shocked by how primitive entertainment in Egypt can be.

"It's been too, too delightful. Exactly like *The Thousand and One Nights*," they stuttered.

The Hostess laughed incredulously. "You are much too

kind. I'm so glad you liked my little house. I did nothing, nothing out of the ordinary at all. As you see, everything was as simple as simple could be."

I did eventually complete my apprenticeship in How To Be a Social Success, and I did master a few essential rules.

I know now that the greeting is the most important part of the ritual. It must be as effusive as possible and contain endless Chéries. In fact, the greeting should be delivered as though you have just arrived from Tibet instead of just next door, and it makes no difference if everybody has seen everyone else at a precisely similar party the night before; it just makes it all the more original.

The conversation should be scintillating at all times and very recherché. For instance, it is a good idea to ask after someone's health and then immediately launch yourself into fascinating details of your own liver condition and cure at Vichy, and it's even better if you can talk with your hands and at the top of your voice so as to drown out the other person. In fact, it's a must.

Should someone ask you, "And how was the première of the film the other night?" you should answer, "The intermission was excellent. I saw Mrs. So-and-So in a blue dress and Mrs. So-and-So in no dress, and Mr. So-and-So with a real So-and-So."

Unless you want to be considered a peasant, you should never, but never, criticize the actors or the action or the script or the production, because you wouldn't have had time to notice if the film was shown upside down and in Kurdish. You would have been far too busy finding out who was sitting in all the loge seats, with whom and wearing

91

what, and after all, that is why you go to the movies in the first place.

When someone admires what you have on, you must immediately reply as you pretend to take it off, "Take it, it's yours." Unless it is a man, there will be loud protests and you'll be safe, and you'll be able to go on to say, "It's only a little dress Jacques Fath made for me." Ditto when somebody admires your little diamond rock, so light you can hardly lift your hand. Just answer that it is a family heirloom your grandmother left you to wear at the beach.

Learn to take things in your stride, like the woman of the world that you are, one who has seen much and really lived. Be like those Lebanese ladies who, even in the depths of their bereavement, did not lose their heads.

It was during a visit of condolence and they were sitting in the salon surrounded by an impressive circle of friends, all in black, all of them sorrowfully and silently sipping coffee. The suffragi came in bearing a little silver tray with a card on it. "Who is it from, Chérie," asked one of the sisters to the one who had taken the card. "Nobody, Chérie," came the answer in a loud clear voice. "Nobody. Just Lady Allenby."

I am by no means as expert as Yvonne and Zeinap, but I do know that when I screech "Chérie, how are you, I haven't seen you in ages," to Sima and Rose at a London cocktail party, everybody turns round to look and then asks aghast, "Oh dear, is that the floor show?"

7

The War Comes To Alexandria

WHEN THE WAR BROKE OUT IN SEPTEMBER, 1939, THE ANGLO-Egyptian Treaty had already ceased to be popular in Egypt and Nahas Pasha, one of its chief originators, was for the time being out of power.

Although the Treaty had stipulated that British forces were to be stationed in the area around the Canal, they were in September, 1939, for one reason or another still very much quartered in the hearts of Cairo and Alexandria, as well as in the immediate vicinity of these cities. This, even in the eyes of the mildest Egyptian, was looked upon as bad faith on the part of the British and an occupation of their country.

Nevertheless, at the outbreak of the war, Aly Maher Pasha, the prime minister, broke off diplomatic relations with Germany and made it clear that Egypt stood and fell wth Great Britain. Martial law was proclaimed and the Egyptian government, in accordance with the Treaty, provided all the facilities in its power, such as the use of ports, airports, and means of communication. In fact, it did all but declare war on the Axis. Whether Egypt should or should not declare war on Germany and later on Italy was much debated at the time. Egypt found herself in the odd position of being neither a neutral, since she was Britain's ally, nor officially at war with Germany and Italy, even when her territory was bombed and penetrated by the Axis. Egypt did finally declare war in 1945, just in time to secure a seat at the Peace Conference.

Both Britain and Egypt realized that whatever contribution Egypt could make in the way of armed forces would not really affect the course of the war one way or the other, and that the most useful thing Egypt could do for the war effort was to place her resources at the disposal of the British. Had the British felt it necessary for Egypt to declare war, no Egyptian government would have dared defy them, for that the British could do what they pleased was unquestionable.

In the winter of 1942, they asked the Italophile King Farouk to dismiss Sirry Pasha, the prime minister, and put Nahas Pasha in his place. When King Farouk, who was never on the friendliest of terms with the Wafd, at first refused, British tanks surrounded Abdin Palace and the British Ambassador threatened to depose King Farouk by force. The king was forced to accede, and Nahas Pasha became prime minister. From then on, even through the blackest days of the war, with Allied defeats resounding in Europe, the Far East, and Africa, with the British civilians and military evacuating Cairo and Alexandria, and when the guns could be heard pounding at Alamein, seventy miles from Alexandria, Nahas and the vast majority of Egyptians stood firm by Great Britain.

That summer of 1939, a few days after the outbreak of the war, we were hurrying back, along with other Alexandrians from the Lebanon, where we had gone instead of to Europe so as not be too far from home. Father had somehow been lucky enough to find a cabin with two berths, which would have to accommodate the seven of us—Mrs. James and Maha were also in the party—on a small but modern Rumanian ship which had recently been put into service. As it turned out, everyone spent the night on deck, crowded to capacity with anxious people hurrying to get home—everyone that is, except Mrs. James and I, who as usual, war or no war, were flat on the two bunks before the ship had even left the harbor.

In Alexandria the sea was as it always is in the fall, very blue and very still, and the sun shone as bright as ever. Mother brought out a tattered old map left over from the First World War and began to mark the Allied positions with little tricolor flags. It was difficult to believe that there was bitter fighting in those countries where we had so light-heartedly holidayed.

Alexandria prepared for a long grim war. Air raid shelters and sandbags were to be seen everywhere. Searchlights streaked the sky. Father came home with some gas masks and Grandmother proceeded to stock up on such essential items as French mustard and asparagus. Rough brown Demerara sugar occasionally appeared next to the smooth white cubes (though even this you could find all through the war). *À la guerre comme à la guerre,* sighed the Alexandria hostess apologetically, as her suffragi passed round a host of delicious things from Baudrot's. It was even rumored that one would not be able to buy meat two days a week, though one would be able to buy all one wished on the preceding days. Tea and oil were also to be rationed, but when one thinks of the strict rationing in England and other countries during and even well after the end of the war, Egypt must surely have appeared a paradise of opulence.

Mother's little tricolor flags seemed to be retreating at an alarming rate, and soon the Swastika was on Paris. The older generation especially were stunned at the downfall of *La France Glorieuse,* where many of them had been educated. They couldn't believe it. Even to the illiterate, Paris, which they had never seen in their lives, was the capital of the universe.

Every evening we'd tune in to the B.B.C., which had acquired the reputation of telling the truth, wondering how much longer the British could go on taking the devastating bombings of the Luftwaffe night after night like that. We all admired British courage tremendously, and the unfailing sense of humor which exploded in programs like "Tommy Handley's Half-Hour." Anxious as she was about her family—her mother, who was ninety-nine, and her seven brothers and sisters, all with three names each, who lived in Coventry—Mrs. James just knew that everything would be all right. She never once considered the possibility of a British defeat.

The majority of Egyptians, too, had nothing but the highest praise and admiration for the way Britain tightened her belt and fought the Battle of Britain against overwhelming odds. Discipline and courage are regarded very highly in easygoing and pampered countries. Except for the war years, I do not remember a time when British Tommies were ever cheered on newsreels shown in Egypt—quite the reverse.

Alexandria was having its own air raids too, mild compared to the blitz, but bad enough for us to spend several nights of that summer of 1940 in the shelter. On one occasion when we came up at dawn after one of the worst air raids of the war, Yvonne found an unexploded bomb which

96

had come right through the terrace and landed on her pillow. Yvonne must have been either unconscious or sleepwalking, for she calmly picked it up and deposited it in the middle of the lawn, where some men came and dismantled it a few hours later.

All over Alexandria, clubs for the armed forces sprang up overnight, and places which had been empty were now crowded to capacity with Allied uniforms. The smart night clubs flourished and the not-so-smart night clubs flourished even more, and as long as a girl had a leg to stand on and could enunciate "Long Live Churchill" she was hired for the floor show.

For the "gally-gally" men who produced fluffy little chicks from inside the Tommies' shirts, these were good days, especially when they sometimes managed to substitute chicks for wallets. Shoeshine boys and vendors of homemade antiques multiplied like flies. Even an old gharry-driver's mare saw life look up, for she was taken to Baudrot's to be fed chocolate éclairs by some Australians so puny looking that it was thought safer to let them have their own way. If one had anything to sell, including one's maiden aunt, this was the time, for Alexandria was booming.

But through it all, wary mammas saw the red light for danger, and down came all the shutters so that daughters would not be lured away by the British Army.

But we were allowed one thing: to go to the military hospitals with ice cream and cakes and cheer up the sick and the wounded, for the mammas' motto was that if a man was in the hospital he was harmless. Cheering up healthy men was considered very loose indeed and not the mission of Nice Eligible Girls.

97

Some years before the War, when we were barely in our early teens, we had formed a little club of our own to help the poor, regardless of their nationality or religion. Now we devoted part of the proceeds of the club to helping those men who were fighting. We bought gifts, made up parcels, and several times a week we met at the home of a Lebanese friend, Isabelle, to sew and knit for the soldiers out in the western desert.

Little by little, and after much persuasion, we were even permitted to entertain at tea groups of convalescents from the Twelfth and Sixty-fourth General Hospitals, for mammas also felt that there was safety in numbers. Regularly, with money from the club, we hired a bus to bring over the men to have tea at one of our houses. More often than not, we entertained them at Isabelle's house. Smaller and newer than the average Alexandrian mansion, devoid of superfluous ornaments and knickknacks, with French windows giving onto a spacious terrace, it was the ideal place for informal and friendly gatherings. Nobody minded when one put one's feet on the chintz-covered sofa, and to me that was the epitome of comfort.

The men came along on crutches or in plaster or with badly burned faces, wearing the bright blue suits and red ties of the hospital uniform and grinning cheerfully as English Tommies do. Occasionally, a too-healthy convalescent would slip in among them and, having spotted Yvonne, Zeinap, Beatrice, and Isabelle, he'd immediately ask to play Postman's Knock. Naturally, the governesses wouldn't let us, and while they kept us on our toes pouring out fresh cups of tea and passing round cigarettes, Mrs. James, Miss

Chalmers, and Isabelle's old Nanny, who was seventy, played the kissing game instead.

Miss Chalmers was Beatrice's governess and the musical one of the group. She was quite incapable of uttering more than two words without bursting into song, the song being "The Isle of Capri."

"Hullo, dear boy," giving him a hearty slap on the back, " 'Twas on the Isle of Capri that I met him," she'd croon, while the rest of us groaned. One thing about people who sing, they're jolly lucky they don't hear themselves. "And how are we feeling today? La, la la la, on the Isle of Capri..."

She was tall and thin, with two enormous front teeth. When she wasn't singing she was playing, and when she did both, it was tragic to everyone but Miss Chalmers, who was positive she was Sophie Tucker and Paderewski rolled into one. With her long neck like a crane's, and her little eyes like a mole's behind the thick glasses which almost touched the sheet of music, she howled, " . . . on the Isle of Capri, hi, hi, hi," while her huge hands crashed down on all the wrong notes.

When "the boys" got well, they went back to their units and we never saw them again, to the relief of our mothers. But many did write, even from prisoner-of-war camps in Germany. Sometimes, they'd send a photograph of their stalag group with a cross to mark where they stood, and we'd pore over the emaciated figure and not recognize it as the one we had known at Isabelle's.

Occasionally, when they had been discharged from the hospital, they'd drop in at Isabelle's place for a cup of tea. They said it was like being home, and I think they enjoyed being bullied by Nanny while they kept their eyes on Isabelle.

For months, we couldn't go to her house without seeing a certain Tony there. After leaving the hospital he had visited once, he had visited twice, and he had visited over and over again. He was a tall gangling sailor who not only appeared to have lost his ship but who seemed to have lost his wits to boot, and though Isabelle was blissfully ignorant of this (and, mercifully, her parents were, too) he was madly in love with her. He was like the furniture in the place and he never said a word. You'd go into the dining room and you'd find Tony blowing smoke rings in a corner. You'd go into the kitchen and you'd find Tony doing the dishes with Mohamed. You'd go into the bathroom and you'd find Tony, so you'd come out again.

Every evening at seven sharp, Nanny handed him his cap and said, "Now be off with you, Lord Nelson," and he'd go.

Then one day, two petty officers came to the house. They were looking for Lord Nelson, who had never gone back to his ship, and they had heard that he came there. Nanny admitted that indeed he had been coming for months. They went in. Lord Nelson was sitting on the stairs, his chin resting in his hands, doing nothing in particular. He went away quietly and we never saw him again, but about two years later he wrote to Isabelle to say that he would never forget her or the club and that he had given her name to his little daughter.

The first casualty among the ranks of the Eligible Girls was Beatrice.

Beatrice was not only uncommonly attractive, she was the cream of Lebanese womanhood, the jackpot, the Most

Eligible Girl in Town. She was tall and willowy, with golden hair and brown eyes which flashed rebellion, and though she was quiet, she had what people call character. Perhaps a little too much character, in fact, for she had very decided opinions. She stood for the weak against the strong, for the poor against the rich, and she was their champion. Perhaps because she had never had any—always being bundled from one place to another in the car with Miss Chalmers—she stood for Freedom with a capital "F," and devoured books on every kind of revolution. She liked to argue, too. If you said white, she said No; if you said black, she said No; if you said No, she said Yes, and above all, she was prepared to fight to the death to marry the man of her choice.

The man of her choice was Captain Ranger, who had infiltrated himself, no one knows exactly how or where, into Beatrice's life, and, moreover, right under the very nose of Miss Chalmers. But even the most vigilant governess is no match for a captain, especially a captain in the commandos whose business is infiltrating. And Captain Ranger was no ordinary commando, for he could write letters to rival Byron's, passionate letters so full of fire that one could have fried an egg on the note paper. She was his moon, his sun, his central heating, his Lebanese lily, whatever that is. It seems his arm still quivered from shaking hands with her. This last was no exaggeration, for the brave Beatrice's handshake was usually enough to dislocate one's arm, and those who knew her well avoided any kind of handshake with her.

That Captain Ranger's grandmother was supposed to have several titles and French blood and that she kept an open house left Beatrice quite unmoved. She was above wealth. But when he told her that all his pay went to support four little orphans he had adopted, together with a woman to look after them, she was moved to tears. Had anyone ever seen such a kind, generous man? "Money, money, money," she cried, "that's all anyone in Alexandria ever thinks of."

When he developed a cough from smoking and told her he was consumptive, he was as irresistible as if he had mentioned six Cadillacs and three oil wells to another girl. Immediately, she knew where her destiny lay. She would marry Steve Ranger, nurse him on his deathbed, and look after the orphans.

The rumor quickly went the rounds of the salons. Beatrice, of all people! Didn't she know, cried the Pekinese, that God had created beautiful girls for civilians like her son Robert, and the British Army for the plain variety? Beatrice and an Englishman—it was unthinkable. Her poor family. What a black day in their life, tsk, tsk, tsk.

While we stood by, on the alert, wondering whether Beatrice's rebellion would bring us more freedom to go and come as we pleased, and maybe even cheer up an occasional healthy man, Beatrice, who was twenty-one, was taking high-handed action and threatening to walk out of the house if she wasn't allowed to marry the Captain. After a brief but terrible battle on the home front, Beatrice's engagement was announced.

There was a large family lunch to introduce the healthy-looking but nevertheless consumptive Captain. It was a sad occasion. Tears were shed over the rolled vine leaves by everyone except the Captain, who was doing rare justice to the Lebanese food.

The Lebanese colony was in tears. "Beatrice, Beatrice," they wailed, as they beat their faces in despair, "how could you do this to us?" Beatrice, she who could have married anybody, or rather *somebody*, to want to go and marry a nobody? It was the Evil Eye, that's what it was. Why, there were the sons of So-and-So, who had millions, and the sons of So-and-So, who would soon have millions, and if she wasn't interested in anyone in Alexandria, there were plenty of nice young men in the Lebanon, all of them Lebanese, and Maronites, too. "What a tragedy," they clucked their tongues, "what a tragedy for her poor family."

But in spite of the engagement lunch, Beatrice was not destined to be either the wife or the widow of the consumptive Captain. Quietly, Beatrice's family had been making a few investigations on the side, which revealed without the shadow of a doubt that Captain Ranger had omitted some very interesting details. He was indeed supporting four children, but far from being adopted, they had been begotten by the Captain himself, and the woman who took all his pay was none other than his devoted wife. The French blood and large house were there all right, only the house had been closed by the police, and as for the grandmother's titles, it was presumed that she had, in her day, been called a few unaristocratic names.

The telephone lines were jammed for a week, and Alexandria buzzed from one end of town to another.

"You see, you see," went the tongues led by the Pekinese, "that's what comes of giving girls too much freedom."

"Didn't we tell you?" mothers scolded their daughters as though they all had Captains up their sleeves as well. "Didn't we tell you mothers know best?"

But the good obedient girls who had been patiently sewing at home bent lower over their petit point, glad that they had never met a captain and serene in the knowledge that their families would soon find the right husband for Nice Girls.

As for the Lebanese colony, it had known all along, of course, about adventurers like Captain Ranger who come especially from the other ends of the earth and make a bee-line for their nice, respectable girls. And because they were so upset—the Lebanese are very emotional, you know—and because they couldn't contain their indignation any longer, they threw "little" coffee parties and "little" tea-parties to make quite sure that everyone had heard the long sad saga of poor Beatrice.

Poor Beatrice, we were very angry with her. But how was she to know about men like the Captain? In her code of honor, when one speaks it is the truth, which everyone will agree isn't just admirable, it's stupid. However, she took it all with a stiff upper lip, like a real trooper.

Life was very grim for us all after that. It was like going back to the Middle Ages. If some poor wretched soldier in a hospital ward so much as gasped for "another cup of tea, please, Miss," the governesses pounced on us and hissed, "Don't you dare go near him, he's another Captain Ranger," or, "Remember what happened to poor Beatrice," as though she had been murdered by Jack the Ripper. Things were really very rough for a long time. "The story of Poor Beatrice," as it was called, ran for months, even longer than did *Gone With the Wind* at the Royal Cinema.

The second casualty was me. I was slushing buckets of ice cream around the ward of the Twelfth General Hospital as usual, daydreaming that I was the Devastating Jacqueline for whom healthy men not only threw parties but sometimes threw themselves out the windows. Yes, as the Devastating Jacqueline who did things for a dress, not the other way around, I had a serious problem, one which was getting quite out of hand: How to keep the men from collapsing over me like a tent. *Men,* ha, ha! They were like streetcars, one every five minutes, only more so. My life was just strewn with them.

"Jacqueline," chorused the Navy, beating a path to my door.

"Jacqueline," cried the Army on bended knees, "give us a break."

"Jacqueline," cried the Air Force, "don't be aloof."

"Jacqueline, what on earth's the matter with you, are you sick?" said Sister loudly. "Why are you fluttering your eyes like that?"

"Oh, oh, er . . . er . . . no, no, I'm fine," said the Devastating Jacqueline.

"Well, if you are sure you're all right," said Sister, peering at me, "would you take this book to Room Five? An American. The book is about fish, of all things. Very sound of the word makes me sick. Thanks, dear."

Carrying my bucket and leaving a trail of dreams and melting ice cream behind me, I arrived at Room Five. There was a card up on the door which read:

CAPTAIN WILLIAM R. CAROL

ARMY AIR CORPS

and underneath, someone had written in pencil, "Jaundice."

I knocked and went in, and that was my Waterloo.

Over There? They're Over Here

As though there weren't enough characters in Alexandria, the Americans had suddenly arrived after landing in North Africa, as quietly as Americans usually arrive anywhere, bringing with them everything from jeeps to juices as well as a large hunk of Texas.

Until then I had not known very much about America because, of course, I had been to the English Girls' College where, in the odd history class fitted in between hockey and lacrosse, the emphasis had been more on the colonies acquired rather than the colonies lost. I did know, however, that when the British left there was a civil war, which is apparently what always happens when the British leave a place.

Of the Americans themselves, I had heard a little more, but it was too terrible for words. It was rumored that they chewed gum, put their feet on the table, and didn't speak English.

"When a person says such things as 'yeah,'" said Mrs. James, stretching one corner of her mouth to her ear, and Mrs. James knew all about Americans, "he has indeed gone to the dogs."

Then too, there was Zeinap, who had been to school in

Washington, and who had come back with a sinister spelling which greatly distressed our headmistress, and the kind of accent which prevented her from being in any of the school plays.

But we were not entirely without our American connection. Every self-respecting Lebanese has a finger in every pie and a relative in Brooklyn. Uncle Farid and his younger brother had left the Lebanon when they were in their teens to seek a fortune in the New World. They needn't have bothered to go quite so far, because the Lebanese are pretty good at making money anywhere. Naturally they prospered, conquered all of Brooklyn, and, after taking stock of American girls, decided they'd be far better off if they took a trip to Lebanon and picked themselves nice, gentle Lebanese brides who wouldn't talk back to them and brought them back to the States.

One year, Uncle Farid, Aunt Salwa, and young Sam— it was the least the family could do to name him after the bounteous American Uncle Sam—had come to the Lebanon to visit all the relatives. We had been there ourselves that summer of 1939 and were thrilled at meeting an American cousin.

There had been innumerable family lunches of a dozen courses each in their honor, and then all the cousins from Damascus to Beiteddin had sat in a large circle in Aunt Louise's and Uncle Henri's garden up at Aley, sipping coffee, eating rose petal jam, talking at the top of their voices, and of course, doing this and that with their hands.

Aunt Salwa had been delighted to be with her kind of people again, for although she had been in the States for about twenty years now, in her mind she had been living in

107

the Lebanon. But Sam was like a fish out of water. We couldn't understand a word he said, except "it stinks," but we did gather that everything was bigger and better in Noo York. He didn't like the food and he didn't like the flies and he spent most of the time in the "john." He only began to show an interest in life when he climbed aboard the U.S. ship which was to take him back to his beloved Noo York. The relatives were very distressed that he seemed to have taken nothing from the Lebanese. "What do you expect, Chérie," they told one another, "that's what happens when you eat out of cans."

But in spite of Mrs. James' withholding her vast knowledge of America from us and our skimping over the American chapters at school, "it was written," as Zeinap says, that I should get to know a great deal more about Americans.

Shortly after the Americans had taken over Alexandria, I received an invitation to the inauguration dance of the American Red Cross. I never knew who sent the invitation, probably the American Consulate, but there was my name properly spelled on the yellow card, and in red letters moreover. I called Sima and Rose to tell them my news.

For several minutes I couldn't figure out what was going on. Somebody was sobbing in the background, there was the angry voice of Big Brother Brj, and Sima herself was jabbering away and making no sense at all. I finally gathered that the uproar was because Sima and Rose had received invitations too.

Obviously, the fact that we had received invitations didn't mean that we would be able to go to this inaugural dance. Fate, all by itself, might arrange for us to attend the closing dance of the Red Cross Club, who knows how many years from now, when we would be so haggard and so un-Eligible our parents would be glad to give us for free to the Marines. But we would have to aid Fate considerably if we wanted to attend this dance only a few days away.

We knew from experience that our parents would have numerous objections. The Red Cross, in spite of its name, was neither a hospital nor a convalescent home, and those Americans would presumably be healthy. "You can't possibly go out and dance with healthy men," cried Mother. Of course, their being American made them twice as healthy and therefore twice as dangerous.

"They dance cheek to cheek," cried Father, appalled. "I won't have my daughter dancing cheek to cheek. Thank God, I'm still capable of making an honest living for my family."

"Anyway, how would you get home?" cried Mother. "You know we never keep the chauffeur out late; the poor man is entitled to some rest."

I decided to confer over the phone with Sima and Rose.

"What does your Father say?" I asked anxiously.

"He says these are healthy men who don't need cheering up," said Sima, "and that he is quite capable of making an honest living for his family."

I asked her what their mother and Big Brother Brj had to say.

Plenty, it seemed. Their mother was still sobbing at having nurtured such depravity, and Big Brother Brj was going to kill them before he'd see his sisters dancing cheek to cheek like those good-time girls he went out with every night.

Things weren't so good.

109

"By the way, if we did go, how would we get back?" I asked Sima.

Sima suggested we might find someone to bring us back in a taxi, so back I went to Mother and Father and said that maybe we could find someone to bring us back in a taxi. "A taxi!" roared Father. "A taxi—I knew it—a taxi, indeed! That's what comes of giving girls too much freedom. Alone with a man in a taxi. What next, I ask you? Did you hear that, Marie? A taxi!"

I stared at Father, amazed at his strange behavior, for being nineteen and very advanced for my age, I was blissfully ignorant of what could happen to a girl in a taxi and couldn't for the love of me understand what all the fuss was about.

And then, when matters stood at their worst, they had suddenly worked out and we had gone along with Sima and Rose's elder married sister, Anny, the former "Angel" whose husband was away on a trip. Anny was simply dying to see real Americans who put their feet on the table, chewed gum, and didn't speak English, so of course she told Brj that she couldn't understand what had gotten into her foolish sisters but she'd sacrifice herself and take them to the dance just this once.

The American Red Cross was housed in a lovely villa in the Greek quarter of Alexandria. A pretty Red Cross girl smiling like a toothpaste ad handed each of us a corsage of red roses as we went in, and said how nice of us to have come.

"How nice of us to have come," echoed that simpleton of a Sima, "why we . . . " when she was literally swept off her feet. We just had time to catch a glimpse of a Sing Sing hairdo and Sima was spirited away.

110

Now Sima was reckoned to be a good dancer. English ballroom, Scottish reels, classical Greek, Armenian folk, she knew them all—but she didn't jitterbug, and the G.I. did. Nevertheless, having got over her first initial shock, Sima was entering into the spirit of the dance—the Indian War Dance, that is. She had the high coloring; all she needed were the feathers. She was jumping first on one foot and then on the other, waving her arms wildly all over the place as though she was about to scalp somebody, and when she wasn't shouting gaily, "Big Apple" (it wasn't), she was sprinting round the room panting, "Where is he, where'd he go?"

I stood paralyzed, watching her, fascinated, and horrified lest the same fate should befall me. My dancing experience, apart from the sailor's hornpipe and the "now imagine that you are gay little trout" sort of thing included in our expensive school curriculum, had been acquired dancing with the convalescents, when, because I was so petite, I invariably found myself hanging from the lapel of the biggest man in the place.

I knew how to do a slow waltz of course. In fact I could do it even slower than the music. Englishmen have a passion for slow waltzes. You hold your partner as far away as possible, and then you lean way back, but not quite all the way over. You must never, never smile, because then people think you are having a good time and it is very un-English to show off. What you must do is stare glassily into space and look as bored as you can, which should be no trouble at all. If you wish, you may engage in sparkling conversation which usually begins with "Have you read any good books lately?"

111

Just then, a Marine with a baby face and tight trousers came over and said, "Dance?" and instead of running away, I said, "Why yeees . . . I'd love to."

I needn't have worried about not knowing the right steps. There weren't any. We could have been dancing on a three-cent stamp. The only thing that moved were his jaws and his hips. I wondered what Father would say if he saw me now. I really must try to make conversation. "Have you read any good books lately?" I asked. "Really good books, I mean?"

This was the magic phrase. With an Englishman it would have worked like a charm and we would have stood in the middle of the floor, not dancing but discussing books, and then we would have been exchanging books for years. But the Marine answered something which sounded suspiciously like, "Naw, I can't read."

"What is your name?" I continued rashly.

"Chuck."

"Oh."

"Where d'you come from?" I persevered.

"The States," he said.

Never mind. I'd been saving my sixty-four-thousand-dollar question for just such a moment as this. This was bound to make him talk and forget about the cheek to cheek.

"Which do you prefer, Alexandria or Cairo?"

He could have answered a thousand and one things. That he preferred Alexandria because it reminded him of Alexandria, Virginia, or that he preferred Cairo because it reminded him of Cairo, Illinois, or again that he preferred Alex because there were fewer flies, or that he preferred Cairo because there were more belly dancers. I knew all

112

this because we had thrashed out the subject over and over again with the convalescents when we couldn't think of anything else to say.

But Chuck just said, "Cairo. Alex stinks."

He continued to sway his hips like a pendulum and then he said, "Say, you British?"

"No, I'm Lebanese."

"You have an awful British accent," he said. "Say, how do you like the Limeys?" he continued.

"The—?"

"The Limeys," he said again.

"Oh. Oh, no, I don't at all; I much prefer the British, don't you?"

Soon after that he'd left in disgust, and Sima and I had gone over to the buffet, which was beautifully arranged, like a page from one of those shiny American magazines. We discovered later on that Americans like to do things well. I'd never seen so many strange salads before, lettuce with—of all things—pears, grated carrot, and mayonnaise; it seemed quite fantastic, but what turned out to be even more fantastic was that we enjoyed it. As for the ice cream, it was the smoothest, creamiest, covered-with-marshmallows ice cream that I have ever tasted. They didn't make it like that in Alexandria.

Except for Sima crying excitedly, "He's asked me to go necking in the garden; it's some kind of an American sport, so it should be fun," the evening went smoothly by. The Marine reappeared and asked me for the last dance.

"Say," he asked, "who's taking you home?"

"Mohamed," I replied.

"Mohamed? He your date?" he wanted to know.

113

"Oh, no, he's Anny's chauffeur," I explained.

"Well, why don't you send him away, and I'll take you home in a cab?" he suggested.

"Thank you," I said, "but there is no need to go out of your way. I live quite far out."

"How far? An hour in a cab?" he leered.

"Oh, no, about fifteen minutes or so, but really, there's Mohamed. It's quite all right."

"Honey," he said, "what's quite all right about Mohamed? I just want to see that you get home safely."

There seemed no other alternative but to tell him the shameful truth. "My parents are very strict and only allowed me to come on condition that I return with Anny's car and chauffeur. I'm not allowed to go out alone."

"But Honey," he said, "you're not alone; you're with me."

"Yes, but you see, my parents are very strict . . . "

Chuck had it all figured out.

"Let me call your parents," he said. "I'll call them right away and we'll have a little talk. What's their number?"

"No, no, please," I begged, wondering what Father would say when the phone rang at this hour and he heard the Marines had taken over.

"You don't know me, Honey," he said. "I have a way with parents."

Yes, I could just see that.

"What's the number, Honey? I'll call them and tell them that I'm taking you home."

There was no other way out, so I made up the first number that came to my head and fled to Mohamed.

Actually, we need not have worried about how we were going to get home, for transportation was provided for the

114

guests, and the Red Cross girl, as she invited us to next week's dance, explained that it would always be available.

"We understand that nice girls are very strictly chaperoned in this part of the world," she said, "and we would like to have nice girls come to our dances, so we're providing transportation for them. I hope you'll be able to come every week."

With that, we became regular visitors to the club. The fact that the Red Cross was in one of the nicest neighborhoods in town carried great weight with our parents and there were surprisingly few parental objections when more and more of our time was taken up with American activities.

Tongues wagged, of course, as they would have done, I fancy, even if we had never moved out of the house. And telephone calls to Mother trebled. But that was Alexandria.

"Marie," the Pekinese would cry. "I saw your daughter Jacqueline bicycling towards the zoo with the whole crew of a battleship behind her. Really, Marie, she'll never find a husband after this."

But Mother would reply that Chérie, it was a destroyer, not a battleship, and nothing could possibly happen to a girl on a bicycle.

The war has been over for many years now, and the Americans have long since returned home, some of them to that other Alexandria in Virginia. But not without leaving behind them their own special brand of civilization. Should you get stranded out in the middle of the Sahara, you can take it from me a suffragi will appear with an ice-cold bottle of Coca-Cola.

9

The Convalescents and
One in Particular

IT WAS FIVE O'CLOCK ON CHRISTMAS EVE AND THE TWELFTH
General Hospital's Ward B looked very festive with its
paper chains and colored lanterns. That morning, the
Friendship Club had come along in full force with all of its
twelve members and six governesses to put the finishing
touches on before the party.

Isabelle had brought along some poinsettias from her
garden. They were often referred to as daughter-of-the-
consul, perhaps after some consul's redheaded daughter.
They had large red petals and long stems and they were very
decorative, but they never lasted very long once they had
been cut and put in water. Adèle, the artist, had sketched
masses of pin-ups with amusing captions underneath each
one, and some of us, Beatrice, Yvonne, and Helen, Sima
and Rose, and Mitzi, an attractive Greek girl whose English
governess was known as the Sphinx, after the gossip magazine, had bustled about with cakes and sandwiches sorting
them out on little plates ready to pass round to those who
wouldn't be able to leave their beds.

The governesses were very excited. This was their war,
their battlefield.

"Have you got the paper hats, Chalmers old girl?" asked the Sphinx, "and the candles for the tree?"

"You haven't forgotten the crackers, have you, Penelope Amanthe Ethel?" asked Isabelle's nanny.

At six o'clock, one of the doctors was to dress up as Santa Claus and distribute the gifts, now safely locked in Sister's room. Some of the gifts we had bought; some of them Mitzi and Isabelle, who were very clever with their fingers, had made themselves.

Miss Chalmers had even had the piano brought over from Beatrice's house, and a little old donkey cart had delivered it for twenty piastres. As soon as the piano had been hauled into the ward, one of the convalescents had gone over and tinkled with the keys. Then, slowly finding himself, he had played everything from Dixieland to Chopin.

Now the party was in full swing, and because Bill was there, it was to my feeble mind the most successful, delightful party I had ever been to. It had been ten days since Sister had asked me to take that book about fish in to him, and I had overstayed then, talking my head off until Mrs. James had come to fetch me and I had jumped up and bolted like a frightened rabbit.

"Come back soon," he had called out, and I had come back every day but one.

When Mother had seemed surprised and said that surely I wasn't going to the hospital again today, I had mumbled something about a poor little American who was on his last legs and who needed cheering up.

Actually, Bill was far from little, being over six feet tall and built on a large scale like everything American, and he didn't look as though he needed cheering up. He seemed

117

most easygoing and relaxed, but of course you could never tell. There was a man in the ward who looked the picture of serenity, and yet he worried so much about the wife he had left behind that he gnawed himself into an ulcer. Some people were like that, Sister said. Well, Bill didn't have a wife, that much I had gathered, but maybe he had a girl. That was as good as being engaged, although while the Americans all seemed to have girls back home, it didn't appear to stop them from having girls over here too. The pigs.

He looked nice, this Bill. Comfortable to be with. His eyes were a very clear blue and the eyelids with black lashes drooped a little at the sides as though to protect their delicate color. Now he was stopping to say something to Miss Chalmers and she was giving him a hearty slap on the back, calling him "my boy," no doubt. He didn't look as though he minded being the only American in the party and he had gone around chatting with everybody, breaking into loud guffaws every now and again. He came over and said, "Would you like to dance?"

"Would you?" I said, my mind more and more feeble.

"Sure—I asked you, didn't I?" he laughed.

"Er . . . cheek to cheek?" I continued, with my uncanny gift for saying the wrong thing at the right time.

"Well, that can be arranged, you know," Bill replied.

"Oh, no, I didn't mean it that way," I explained. "It's immoral, you know."

"Really," he said, raising an eyebrow, his blue eyes very blue. "You tell me."

"I'm not going to tell you another thing. You only laugh at me."

The day before, Bill had been very amused when I had told him how strictly chaperoned I was, and he had made me pea-green with envy with tales of young people in the States who went out without being trailed by governesses. When a girl had a date, she introduced the boy to her family and then they both went out together. No need for pleading or deceit, or having to move escorted by another three couples. Out here in Egypt, one didn't go out with a young man unless one was engaged, and even then, one was usually heavily chaperoned.

Bill suddenly said, "I'm leaving the hospital next week. Going back to Payne Field, Cairo."

"That's nice," I said. I didn't think it was nice at all; I thought it was awful.

"I was wondering whether we couldn't have lunch together someplace on Wednesday. I don't have to go back to Cairo until the evening. What do you say?"

"No, er . . . I couldn't possibly," I said.

"Not even possibly?" he went on. The devil take those blue eyes.

"Er . . . no, my parents wouldn't allow me to . . . "

"Would it do any good if I talked to your family?" Bill asked.

"Oh, no, really, it would be fatal," I said.

Someone was playing "White Christmas." Everyone began to sing and all those who were able to move gathered round the piano. Whenever that tune was played, everyone always joined in. It reminded them of home, I suppose, and their families sitting round the fire, and all the Christmas cards on the mantelpiece. We had tried to make the ward look Christmassy with the big tree glistening with tinsel and plenty of cotton wool to look like snow. But outside, there was no snow, only beautiful Egyptian sunshine, and it was like a spring day in England. Yesterday some of us had gone to the beach. It had been deserted, as it always is in December, but the sea, though cold, was calm and transparent, and Beatrice had gone in for a swim.

" . . . just like the ones I used to know."

Nanny's "boy," Johnny, his burned face still wound in bandages, lay in bed, his head leaning back against the wall, motionless, and the man next to him, surrounded by his pictures of pin-ups, sat quietly for once, blowing smoke rings. I looked round the ward at all the faces. Miss Chalmers was singing better than usual. She had lost her fiancé during the First World War and still wore the artillery medal he had given her, and Mrs. James, whose husband had died on the battlefield during that earlier war, seemed to be gazing out the window at nothing in particular. And Sister, so brisk and so efficient—I wondered what her story was. They were singing, but their faces, as all the faces in the ward, had softened, and some of them, it was quite obvious, were miles and miles away.

Miss Chalmers broke the spell by taking over at the piano and crashing into the opening bars of "Sir Roger de Coverley." It was one of the pieces she played best, and the men and the girls quickly formed two lines facing each other and one couple at a time swung down between the two rows to the accompaniment of hands clapping. The nostalgic moment had passed. Mrs. James was squealing like a schoolgirl as she was swung round and round by a hefty man with a red beard. Sister looked briskly about her and went over to have a word with Bill. The man with the pin-ups sat up holding his one good leg, laughing, and there was a smile on Johnny's face. It was strange how music could make and unmake a mood.

The dancing continued gaily for another half-hour or so, and then it was time for "Auld Lang Syne," which we sang, hand crossed over hand like a chain, in the middle of the ward. The minute it was over, one of "the boys" called for three cheers for the Friendship Club, which made me so self-conscious I didn't know where to look. Miss Chalmers promptly replied with three cheers for "the boys," and the party was over.

As we were walking down the corridor to leave, Bill said, "Look, if you've got a spare moment tomorrow, why don't you drop by?"

We always went to church on Christmas Day, after which we visited all the distant and not-so-distant aunts and uncles and cousins. There would be a large family lunch at Grandmother's place, and in the afternoon we would stay home, because the relatives would in their turn be visiting us. Taking all this into consideration, I said I wasn't doing a thing and would definitely be dropping by.

When I arived home, Mother was in the middle of dressing, for there were to be about fifty people to dinner tonight. Karim and his family, Beatrice and her younger sister Marguerite, and Robert the Eligible, among others.

I was a little concerned about Robert these days. From one or two hints which the Pekinese had dropped about as subtly as a club, I had gathered that the list of suitable wives for Robert had narrowed down to one: me. I was not looking forward to the evening. Robert was all right in his own way, but he was a crashing bore and I wasn't in the least interested in hearing about the ups and downs of cotton. I had my own to worry about. Sometimes, I could imagine myself married to Robert, with whom I had nothing in common, living with cotton day in and day out, and getting a little more bored each year, while people would say, "There's an excellent marriage for you, and he's on the board of simply everything, Chérie."

"Mother," I said quickly, "you know that poor little American who has been very ill in the hospital?"

"Is he dead?" asked Mother.

"No, no, he's better, and he's going back to Payne Field on Wednesday, probably to get killed." Dead on his feet in the Long Bar at Shepheard's was more likely. "Don't you think it would be nice to have him over to lunch before he goes away?" I asked.

Mother put a drop of perfume behind each ear and said, "Why don't you ask your Father, Dear?"

Father had already dressed and was taking some clock to pieces, after which it would work so well it would have to be replaced, like all the things Father repaired.

"Father," I began, "you know that poor little American who has been so ill ... "

"Is he dead?" asked my Father.

"No, no, he's better and he's leaving soon. Do you think we could have him over to lunch—to cheer him up, you know?" I lied.

"Well," Father said, "as long as he's sick, he's safe, I suppose. But how many other convalescents were you thinking of having?"

"Oh, only this one."

122

"Only one? Why one? Is he the only one who is sick?" Father asked suspiciously.

"No, no, of course not, and he's not as sick as he was. I just thought it would be nice to ask him to lunch. He is so far away from home and everything," I explained, carefully omitting the fact that Bill had asked me to lunch first.

Mother came in and said, "I think it would be all right if you could invite a few more from the hospital, don't you agree, George?" Father said yes, he supposed so, and it occurred to me that Mother's suggestion was not such a bad one. If there were a few more convalescents and if I asked some of my friends, the atmosphere would be more relaxed. It would be fun.

During the whole evening I thought of Wednesday, and was in such an exuberant mood and so enthusiastic over every cotton yarn Robert was spinning that I realized afterwards I would only have myself to blame if a proposal from Robert's mother, the Pekinese, came before New Year's Day.

Wednesday rolled round, and Rose and I went along to the Twelfth General Hospital to fetch Bill and the five convalescents. They were all waiting downstairs and my heart sank at the sight of Bill. Except for his hair, which appeared to have been hit by a runaway lawn mower, he not only looked very fit, he looked very good in his uniform. It was the first time I had seen him in anything but the blue hospital outfit. The jacket sat easily on his big shoulders, the buttons shone, the silver wings looked imposing above a row of ribbons, and the right crease was in the trousers. He looked like a general. I hoped he would have the sense to tell

Mother how ill he was still feeling. "Hi," he said, "what's new?"

I stammered something quite unintelligible and we all piled into the cars. We took the road along the Corniche. In summer it was always very crowded with streams of cars, people strolling about in their bright pajamas, and Arabs grilling corn on their little charcoal fires, but at this time of the year it was almost deserted, though the sky was still blue and the sun pleasantly warm. The casinos jutting out into the water were closed now and already seemed to be in need of a new coat of paint after the few violent storms which Alexandria occasionally gets in the wintertime. We turned right, up the road with the flame trees which were not flowering now, and into the drive.

The wicker chairs were out on the lawn and everybody was there—Mother, Father, Mrs. James and Miss Chalmers, Sima, Beatrice and Helen, but not Yvonne, who was lunching with Karim and his family. Mrs. James took over and introductions went off easily, "Mama, Papa . . . You know Lofty Jones, of course," she said.

"Of course," said Mama and Papa, who had never set eyes on the man before. "And this, Mama," she continued, "is my Australian boy. I know Christchurch very well indeed. Oh, is that New Zealand? I was there in 1911, you know. I know New Zealand like the back of my hand, and of course I shall be sixty next birthday, my boy."

She trotted round the Commonwealth, her eyes twinkling like mad. "And this is Bill, Mama and Papa, my American boy. You be careful, my boy, don't you think you're well because you're leaving the hospital. I had a friend, or rather my sister Valerie Jennifer Emma did, who died of jaundice.

He was in the Air Force too. Used to drink himself stupid."

Bill laughed that boisterous roar reminiscent of a good-natured lion, and I sat down as far away from him as possible. I heard Mother say sympathetically, "So you're the American who has been so ill."

I strained my ears to hear what Bill would say.

"Well, Ma'am," replied that clot of a Bill, "it was only a very mild case of hepatitis. In fact, I rather enjoyed it, and now of course, I feel just great."

"Oh, great," I thought.

"Really, you feel well?" asked Mother, apparently very surprised to hear it. Her eyes were like Bill's, only more innocent. "I must admit you look very fit, although," she added to my relief, "you should be very careful what you eat for a long time. Mrs. James is right, hepatitis can be very nasty." When Mother got hold of a subject, she liked to work it to death, like Father with his home repairs.

"I suppose," she continued, "that that is why they cut all your hair off like this. They did it to me when I had typhoid, but it grows again, thicker and better, so don't worry."

Across Mrs. James, who was telling her story of the native who gave her a kiss instead of cheese with the hysterical laughter that always accompanied it, I heard Bill say that it wasn't really because of the hepatitis, Ma'am, but that Americans often cut their hair like that so that the bugs wouldn't get into it. Well, I thought, if the man wants to be a diplomat he should give up telling the truth quite so bluntly.

His eyes were really very blue, almost transparent, like the sea around the Greek Islands. It was difficult not to

125

notice them, but they looked especially attractive today. It was probably the beer.

The conversation flowed easily and pleasantly and a gentle breeze swept through the drooping branches of the mimosa trees. Basking in the sun like this, with the sound of the pigeons billing and cooing, the war seemed very far away, though it wasn't really, and in fact it had brought us these men who were sitting here in our garden drinking beer. That was Fate. It had nothing to do with our willing it, or with the men's wanting to be here. They probably never dreamed of leaving their own country, except Bill, who said that as a child he'd spin the globe round and bringing his finger down on some distant land would think: "Some day, I'm going to be right there."

Well, here he was, in one of these distant lands. I wondered if this was what he had expected Egypt to be like. Maybe all that he had known about it was that it had some Pyramids and that rich tourists went there in the wintertime. We had met a much-traveled English couple in Germany once, who had asked us if we had gas and electricity in the houses in Egypt. We had been terribly shocked at their ignorance, but it was true, I supposed, that the fellaheen in the mud huts didn't have either.

Mrs. James was floating in the Caribbean in a trunk when Gamal, wearing a red and gold outfit, came along to say that lunch was ready. The house felt chilly after the warm December sun, but a nice log fire was blazing in the dining room, and with the little tree on the table and the crackers, it felt Christmassy. Lunch went off very well. Father had by now discovered that the Australian also liked to fix radios and the two of them were going to have a session after lunch.

126

Mrs. James was losing her pants winning the set at Wimbledon. Mother was cheering Bill, whom she was calling Colonel, by giving him a long list of all the things he wouldn't be able to eat for the next five years, and the outspoken Beatrice shattered us all by saying, "I just love life with a capital F." It seems she meant Freedom and not what the two one-track minds on either side of her thought she meant.

The crackers were pulled, the corny jokes read. We put on the paper hats and drank to a speedy end to the war. After coffee in the garden, Father and Australia went in to repair the radio, Mother disappeared to have a quick siesta, and—leaving the others to play croquet—Bill suggested I show him the tadpoles in the pond at the bottom of the garden.

When it was time for the convalescents to leave, Mother surprised me by asking if I wouldn't like to show Colonel Carol some of the sights of Alexandria before he caught his train. When, with rather too much alacrity, I agreed that it was an excellent idea, she immediately added that, of course, all the other girls were to go along as well.

We set off, Beatrice, Sima, and Rose in the back, Bill in the front, and me driving. Driving was one of the few things Father approved of for girls. Anwar, the latest of our chauffeurs, had again taken the afternoon off to attend a wedding, for Anwar went to as many weddings as Elsa Maxwell, and Father had more than a sneaking suspicion that most of the weddings existed only in Anwar's imagination. But he was a nice man, always laughing, and it was difficult to get angry with him.

After an animated discussion in Armenian which I was

127

quite unable to understand but which included the words "Bill" and "Jackie" several times over, Sima and Rose inquired with their customary eloquence if we didn't think they were *de trop*.

"Hey, you two, you don't want us two along too, do you?"

Naturally, Bill and I protested that no, no, by all means, their company was always a treat, especially on Bill's last afternoon in Alexandria, but they finally asked to be dropped off at the Sporting Club. I said I'd be back to fetch them later. Beatrice decided to get out as well and take a brisk walk round the golf course so that she could think about what that other word could be which also began with "F."

We drove quietly along the Corniche away from Ramleh towards Ras-el-Tin Palace and the Yacht Club. Unlike Cairo, which, though cosmopolitan, teems with Eastern atmosphere, there wasn't much to see in Alexandria. True, there were the Catacombs, the Greco-Roman Museum, and the Antoniadis Gardens, but that wasn't the real Alexandria. The familiar sights were not so much Pompey's Pillar as the pompous Mohamed Aly Club where the prosperous pashas and businessmen sat on their balcony overlooking Rue Fouad staring gloomily at everything about them. Alexandria undoubtedly had a charm of its own, a certain "something," but it didn't hit one. It was far more subtle and far more pervading. It was in the little streets of Ramleh with their sweet scent of honeysuckle, in the smooth summer nights loud with the weird voices of frogs, even in the sad passé-looking buildings downtown. Alexandria, once the city of Alexander the Great, now no more than a Mediterranean port, exercised a very melancholy and very real fascination.

We were coming to Anfouchy with its fish market, and passing through the less salubrious part of Alexandria. On a corner of the beach, disfigured old boats dried in the sun, and children in rags and pajamas flew their homemade kites with youthful abandon as they walked straight into the on-coming cars. A tram swung out of a side street and onto the Corniche, but I did not dare overtake it, for people clung to it like grapes to a vine, and I knew they were in the habit of jumping off without so much as glancing behind them. Two youths raced up madly, and, having caught the tram, crouched precariously on the bumpers, laughing. The sea just beyond was blue and still, and a very dark-skinned man stood on a reef, water up to his ankles, a basket on one arm, a rod in the other, fishing.

The road again straightened out and widened, the tram disappeared, and so did the children, the noise, and the foul buildings with their washing hanging outside the windows. We passed by Ras-el-Tin Palace and its smartly clad guards and came to the Yacht Club.

It was one of the spots I liked best in Alexandria, quiet and peaceful, with a magnificent view of the harbor and lighthouse, and the tea was always plain but good: hot buttered toast and apricot jam, English biscuit and fruitcake. Hardly anyone came at this time of the year, but one quick look and I recognized the Pekinese's car and chauffeur in the otherwise deserted parking lot. She was probably there with her friend the Bulldog, waiting to pounce on just such a piece of juicy gossip as the sight of George and Marie's daughter with a Man Who Was Not A Lebanese. That did

129

it. I turned the car round quickly, determined to put as many miles as possible between the Pekinese and myself. My reputation would be able to stand up and walk the streets of Paris by itself if I were seen going in there alone with this healthy specimen from the hospital.

Where to now? Where could we possibly go? And then I knew. Abukir. We would go to Abukir. No one ever went there.

"Bill," I said, "have you ever heard of Abukir, where Nelson defeated the French in the year I-don't-know-which?" Bill said sure, in the year 1798, and I replied, "Oh. Well, that's where we're going. Nobody, but nobody ever goes there in the wintertime. You'll see."

We sped down the Abukir Road, past the Sporting Club and Sidi-Gaber station, where Bill would be taking his train, and continued straight on where the road split into two by the Summer Palace. Karim's parents had invited us here one evening and the place had been full of British naval officers. The Auberge of the Summer Palace was the place to come to, and people flocked to hear Marco Baben and his violin in his amusing rendition of "Lili Marlene" in Arabic. We crossed the railway lines by Victoria College, now transformed into the Sixty-fourth General Hospital, leaving the boys to manage as best they could in down-at-heel old San Stephano Casino, and soon we were passing Mandara, with fields on either side.

Small, narrow-minded Alexandria was far behind now and Bill and I were talking nineteen to the dozen, almost as incoherently as Mrs. James, and all the windows of the car were open and one of the fields was the greenest green I had ever seen. A water buffalo bathed in the canal alongside the road, a Bedouin woman bent over and filled her earthen-ware jug with the same brown water, and some barefooted kids ran out yelling from a mud hut, chasing geese.

Bill laughed, the smoke from his cigarette whirled madly and blew out the window, palm trees stood out against the pale blue of the winter sky. Blindfolded, a water buffalo slowly turned the water wheel round and round and a man on a donkey turned to look at the speeding car. It was almost cold with the windows open and my hair was blowing all over the place, but I didn't care.

Presently, the road narrowed, its bumpy surface forcing me to slow down. R.A.F. men walked in orderly fashion by the side of the road and a few jeeps and trucks slowed down our progress even more. Then they turned off in the direction of the airfield and with the car raising a cloud of dust, we jogged into Abukir.

It was a sprawling, colorful village, its roads mere tracks of sand, its houses squat and whitewashed, huddled close together and interspersed with the local cafés. The men appeared to be fishermen. They wore pleated baggy trousers rolled up to the knee, a sash around the waist, and various odd scarves tied round their heads. They took no more than a fleeting look at the car, but the ragged, bright-eyed kids ran behind us shouting, "*Gambari, gambari,*" as they held up enormous shrimps in each hand.

We proceeded slowly through Abukir, catching a few brief glimpses of the sea in between the houses. Then we turned away from the village proper and suddenly found ourselves looking down onto Abukir Bay. A multitude of fishing boats rested peacefully all along the water's edge, their thick

131

brown nets hanging on the masts to dry, and to the east were sugary white sand dunes.

"Isn't that really something," said Bill. It was one of those beautiful afternoons typical of Egyptian winters, when the light is so clear that it is difficult to imagine such a thing as mist, let alone fog. The sun, that eternal topic of European conversation, looked down warmly, and happy little clouds flitted across the sky. Rain was the last thing they had in mind.

They had no sooner spotted the car than the fishermen and their children, who had been quietly repairing their nets and chatting by their boats, rushed over to us, their hands full of fish. Now I love fish—the *meunière* or thermidor kind—but I don't care for the sight of it in agony, its glassy eyes staring at me from a big palm thrust under my nose through the car window. Bill apparently did, however.

"What do you call these in English?" he kept repeating, "this one, this one here, look."

"This called fish, Sair," chorused the men, "Americani fish, berry good, berry lubly fish," and Bill prodded the fish and wondered if the small ones—didn't anyone really know what they were called—might get used to living in that aquarium he would one day have right in the middle of his living room, if he could get them used to fresh water, of course—what do you think? And he should really go down to the Red Sea some day—apparently there are some beautiful specimens there, clown fish, too, they say, around the coral reefs.

Then he stopped soliloquizing and said, very pained, "Do you mean to tell me that you don't know what those things are called and you've lived with them all your life?"

132

The fishermen, showing their white teeth, which made a mockery of scientific cleaning three times a day, stood grinning and laughing, for Egyptians have happy dispositions and laugh easily, especially at crazy Americans.

After a while, Bill lost interest in the nameless fish, but the men didn't lose interest in Bill, because he was distributing cigarettes all round, and they suggested that the Captain and the Lady (who, if the Pekinese saw her, would be referred to as anything but) should take a boat out to Nelson's Island, or visit Napoleon's fort—which we could see from here—and maybe have their fortunes told in the sand.

Suddenly an imposing figure in a flowing white robe and turban broke through the crowd and opened my side of the car. With a broad smile and a grand sweep of the hand, he said, "Don't listen to those sons of dogs. My Hitler and Mussolini are waiting for you, Sair, and you, Lady."

Bill and I burst out laughing at the sight of his little gray donkeys, their necks festooned with blue beads, little pink bows in their manes, and their saddles covered with red velvet. Without another word, we got out of the car and hopped onto the backs of Hitler and Mussolini. "Go!" cried our guide, and off we trotted down the beach along the water's edge, past all the boats, our guide following a short distance behind, running lightly, his feet hardly making a sound.

The white clouds appeared to race each other across the sky. Bill laughed that laugh which seemed to come from his boots, and I noticed that his feet were nearly touching the ground. The indefatigable guide kept up a stream of anecdotes, half in Arabic and half in English, which he claimed to have got from Napoleon's mouth, and I was laughing too, not making any sense at all, as I tried to hold my skirt down in ladylike fashion and not drop my bag or lose the car keys. But I did drop the bag after all, and the guide picked it up for me and then carried it while he ran. The air was fresh and salty and Mussolini was trotting as fast as his little legs would carry him, and again I had that wonderful feeling of exhilaration and lightheartedness I had had in the car.

The Zephyrion Casino stood overlooking the sea on the north side. It was no more than a large wooden shack, crudely painted in green and yellow, with unattractive brown chairs and tables. But, although it was empty, it had atmosphere, and I could not help hoping it would not be replaced by some showy new construction.

We did not sit inside, sheltered from the wind, but on the terrace looking out over the water. The old Greek waiter, in black trousers and a white jacket which looked as though it had been slept in, emerged from the depths of the casino, rubbing his hands, whether because it was cold or because he was happy to have customers, I couldn't tell. Bill and I said we'd have coffee.

"Coffee?" cried the waiter. "Two nice people like you? You come to Abukir to drink coffee? But you can drink coffee anywhere, not so?" he asked in that accent which pervades every language a Greek speaks. "Don't you want to have some nice grilled shrimps, just like lobsters, as big as this?" He put his hand up to his elbow. "Or maybe soles, very fresh, each one like this? Come, I show you and you choose what you like. Coffee no good, ha, ha."

We followed, quite powerless to resist, and peered into the icebox. The glassy eyes of the fish did not bother me nearly so much now.

134

"Bill," I said, "remember the hepatitis." So Bill remembered—and ordered shrimps, crabs, red mullets—"just to see what they're like"—a bottle of beer, and lots of little hor d'oeuvres.

It was a wonderful meal. The sky was red and pink now because the sun was getting ready to go down, but the sea was restless. Time was running out fast. As we got up to leave, I noticed a couple sitting right inside the casino. I had not seen them before, so they must have just come in. They were leaning across the table, the man talking animatedly, the girl all ears. It was Robert the Eligible with a most un-Eligible girl. For the first time in my life, I felt some sympathy for him. I couldn't help smiling at the thought that he was no more interested in me than I was in him, and that he too had to come to Abukir to get away from the Pekinese and her friends. He lifted his head and saw me with Bill. He looked surprised and then he smiled.

We got into the car. It was quite dark now and we were subdued driving back toward Alexandria. I suddenly remembered Beatrice, Sima, and Rose and hoped that they had had the sense not to wait for me. I turned right, past the Sixty-fourth General Hospital and onto the Corniche. It was deserted and the wheels swished on the damp surface. You could see the pale blue lamps dimly, in a haze almost the whole length of the Corniche, for the blackout had relaxed now that the war was in Italy.

My face felt flushed from all the air at Abukir, and the moon was nowhere in sight to look at its white reflection on the water, which lay in darkness, black and unfriendly, but the myriad stars seemed to beckon and wink and I wished I knew their names.

135

A few drops of rain appeared on the windshield and were followed by more. Perhaps tonight the wind would rise and howl around the garden keeping us all awake. Whenever it poured on an important occasion, like a wedding, for instance, Maha always said it was the Heavens expressing their pleasure and showering down gifts, but then Maha was full of superstition. Nevertheless, I couldn't help wondering whether the Heavens approved of Bill.

There were few people at Sidi-Gaber Station, and it was drafty and cold. It seemed like the middle of the night, but the clock said 8 P.M.

"Don't worry," said Bill, "I'll get weekend passes and come down often."

"Who's worrying?" I said, and to prove that I wasn't, a Niagara of tears streamed uncontrollably down my face.

When I arrived home, the lights were blazing in the downstairs salon and Yvonne rushed up to tell me that the Pekinese had just left after having formally delivered a proposal of marriage on behalf of Robert the Eligible.

10

Lebanon—A Great Little Country

As he said he would, Bill came down to Alexandria almost every weekend, and his plan of attack was just another proof of American ingenuity.

On his first weekend he called Mother and said, in tones as sweet as maple syrup, "You were so kind to me when I had hepatitis, inviting me to lunch, having your daughter show me the sights of Alexandria. I enjoyed that very much, by the way. That's why I feel you'll understand if I ask you a favor."

"What is it?" asked Mother, who, of course, prided herself on being very understanding.

"Well," Bill said, "when I was over at your house, I noticed that you had a piano, and I was wondering whether you would let me practice on it, when I came down from Cairo.

"I am very fond of music and we have no piano where we are based in Cairo," he added sadly.

Mother, who was very soft and almost in tears at the thought of a pianist without a piano, exclaimed, "Of course, you poor man. Oh, what a terrible war this is. Of course, come anytime, anytime at all, and play as long as you like. My husband and I are never at home in the afternoon, so you won't have to worry about being a nuisance."

137

Father, who was not so soft, said to Bill when he turned up, "Look, Captain er . . . er . . . (Father could never remember names) , you come, you play, you finish, you go, no funny businesses with my daughters."

"You must excuse him," said Mother to Bill, "my husband's English is not very good."

"My English it is excellent," retorted Father. "I told to him he can play with the piano and not with my daughters."

Bill said of course, of course, he understood perfectly. When Mother and Father left, I said to Bill, who was poking around the piano, "I didn't know you played."

"I don't," Bill replied, "but this is a good time to learn."

For weeks, Bill came down on Saturday afternoon, fooled around with some scales which were agonizing to listen to at first, but which after a while began to have a definite honky-tonk beat about them, and then left again on Sunday. Halfway through his improvisations, we'd have tea in the garden. Yvonne would discreetly go round to Karim's, and Helen would take Mrs. James to a movie. Sisters are so understanding and co-operative. I was glad I wasn't in Sima's and Rose's shoes, with a brother like Brj, who stood over them whenever they spoke on the phone, snooped around their closets in search of diaries, and generally exhibited remarkable FBI tendencies.

Some six months later, when Bill's piano-playing not only showed no signs of letting up but when we were playing *à quatre mains,* Mother and Father suddenly decided that what I needed was a holiday, and we all took off for Lebanon.

Lebanon is a tiny country whose one and a quarter million people are Christians, Moslems, and Druses, all of them warm-blooded, hotheaded, and very, very friendly. The

Druses are akin to the Moslems, but don't ever tell a Druse that he is like anybody else. Though there are far fewer Druses than there are Moslems or Christians in Lebanon, their political influence has been strong.

While Lebanon is a small country stretching some 120 miles along the Mediterranean and about 35 to 50 miles wide, I hasten to add that except for its size, it is a country where everything is carried out on a large scale. Even the banknotes of small denominations are as large as tents and can be used for blankets. It is of the utmost importance to know that nothing is ever small in Lebanon. The Lebanese think big and talk big. They do not believe in understatement like the British—and quite rightly: look where it has got the British. If you wish to say that Lebanon is a beautiful country, you should say, as the Lebanese do, that it is the most beautiful country in the world, otherwise they will think that you don't like it. You should also say, for instance, when you behold the magnificent Cedars of Lebanon, that now that you have seen them, poor old Mont Blanc looks exactly like an ice cube.

The main occupation of the charming, hospitable Lebanese, whether they live in Beirut, Brooklyn, or Rio, is making money. This, of course, is true of most people, but it is even truer of the Lebanese, and they are very successful at doing this, which is why Lebanon is booming. Others may get to the moon first, but I am sure that a Lebanese will get all the business there.

The Lebanese hobbies are eating and playing cards, the relaxation a little bit of fighting and shooting up in the hills. Clan fights clan, but they all unite to fight the government. That's the most popular sport of all. And they are so sentimental that when they see a beautiful red rose they immediately turn it into jam.

The Lebanese, who are nothing if not enterprising, have spread to the four corners of the earth, not only to show people how to make money, but to tell the world about Lebanon—that the scenery there is of course the most beautiful in the world, that the climate is the best in the world, and that the Lebanese fruits are the juiciest, and especially the biggest, in the world. And what's more, it's all true.

The Lebanese who have made good in the New World or the Old World, or even made the most of the two worlds, usually pay at least one visit to the old country to see how their relatives and friends have fared. Imagine you are one of them. You plan to take the relatives by surprise, but the only one who is going to be surprised is you, for having been away such a long time, you have forgotten how things really work.

Somehow, the word has got around—and this is what you had forgotten—that the son of Aziz or Selim or Habib and his dear family are coming to visit, and the tom-toms have started beating the glad tidings round the hills and everyone is waiting for you at the quayside or the airport and there is no hope of entering unseen. You may try and sneak in if you wish, but someone you have never seen before in your life will rush up to you, arms outstretched, and hail you as his brother, his beloved cousin, or his beloved cousin's cousin, and tell you that everything he has is yours—and for all you know, this may very well be.

Even your favorite aunt who smells of rose water and who you were only going to call the day before you left Beirut is there at the quayside and everyone is shouting at the top of his voice, fighting over you and arguing about who is going to have the honor of inviting you to lunch first. By the time everyone is hoarse, especially you, the matter has been settled and you are whisked away to what Cousin Charlotte calls her little shack up at Aley, which is so little she doesn't know if you'll be comfortable, really. So you think, poor old Charlotte, things have gone badly for her while I've been making money in New York and she's living in some poor wooden hut with outside johns, but you soon discover that the shack bears a startling resemblance to a palace. Cousin Charlotte doesn't agree with you and maintains that it is only a shack, and she is almost in tears because the cook is ill and she hasn't had time to prepare a nice dinner, the kind she knows you are used to having. It's only going to be a snack, potluck, you know, but we are so happy to see you and do tell us about New York. Is it true that you can pay as much as five dollars for a steak she asks, as she piles your plate with lobster.

"Lobster?" you exclaim. "I didn't know there were lobsters in Lebanon."

"No," your hostess replies serenely, "but there is Air France."

So after pouring down the arrack and swallowing about fifty different kinds of hors d'oeuvres—for, after all, Cousin Charlotte did say that there was nothing for dinner, potluck, you know, a snack, a sandwich—you are led to a buffet which looks as though it could feed the whole population of Lebanon. And you also remember that it is going to look very bad if you don't have two helpings of everything. Finally, you have coffee and indigestion, but Cousin Charlotte says that the next time you come, she'll have a proper dinner for you.

141

And now, a word about the service taxis, the only transportation worth mentioning in Lebanon. There are hundreds of such taxis all over Beirut and they go up to the mountains and back continuously, picking up passengers on the way. You may find yourself next to an overweight housewife with baskets of fruit, a Maronite priest, an American tourist, and an A.U.B. student, and the price of the ride is very cheap. But the regular taxis, which like the service ones are mostly brand-new American cars or Mercedes' spouting Diesel fumes, are expensive. Beirut must be one of the easiest places in the world to get about in because the service operates in the center of town as well. All you have to do is stand at a corner and a service taxi will screech to a stop and carry you off, even though all you wanted was just to cross the street. But whether you ride a service or a regular taxi, you will find it a terrifying experience, because the drivers all drive like maniacs, with one hand out the window, the other giving you back your change, and the head turned back to see if you are happy—and you'd better be, because if you're not, they'll sing along with the music on the radio and never look at the road again. The song usually has to do with a girl's eyes. (Incidentally, the Lebanese men have theirs all over the place.) Surprisingly enough, there are fewer accidents than one would expect. This is because most of the chauffeurs have a string of blue beads hanging over the mirror to keep the Evil Eye away. The Evil Eye also operates in Lebanon, and, like everything else, on a large scale.

Beirut from the air is an incredible sight, just as Beirut is an altogether incredible place. First, there is the very

142

bright blue of the Mediterranean with crisp white waves crashing—slowly, it seems from the air—onto a narrow strip of white sand. Rich red earth dotted with clumps of pines appears next. Then comes the city itself, a conglomeration of pale pastel buildings of all shapes and sizes all thrown together untidily in every direction. Beyond the city, like some stage décor, are the mountains of Lebanon, with diminutive houses dotted all over them.

The plane dipped its wing and as I looked out the window, I saw Beirut's tiny harbor with little warships arranged around it like toys. A short distance beyond it, sitting squarely right on the water's edge, was the St. George Hotel and the yachts sailing gaily past it. We circled slowly, taking in a bird's-eye view of the beaches, the splashes of green in the midst of the red soil, the barren purple mountains.

The plane touched down on the Tarmac and the next thing I knew we were coming out into the glare and walking straight into the arms of brigade upon brigade of relatives. The noise of kissing was quite fantastic. The airport building was not as it is nowadays, up-to-date and equipped with juke box and Coca-Cola machine, and the customs shed was the usual mixture of confusion, excitement, and genuine friendliness.

"Shall I open my suitcase?" I asked a cousin who was standing near me, more for something to say than anything else.

"Open your suitcase?" he echoed, appalled. "You are in Lebanon. It would really be the end if they were to look into suitcases now." He thought I was nuts.

As soon as we got out of the customs area, the relatives all cried, "Now we can really kiss you properly," and they started pounding our cheeks all over again. Eventually, exhausted, we all piled into the cars and proceeded to the St. George, where we had planned to spend a few days before going up to Sofar. We were followed by the relatives, very upset that Mother and Father had insisted on staying at a hotel instead of with them. "Though, of course," they chorused, "we know that our miserable little home at Souk-el-Gharb can't possibly compare with the St. George." They were very pained, but they felt better when, an hour later, after we had checked in at the St. George, we were sitting down to lunch at Ajami's.

Ajami's is one of the institutions of Beirut. It is one of those places which one hears so much about but which is a shock when one sees it for the first time because it is so ugly and shabby. But like so many ugly and shabby places the world over, the food there, if you care for Lebanese food, is excellent.

It was a long narrow room, like a corridor, with bare walls and a crudely tiled floor. A couple of voluble waiters in black trousers and rolled-up shirt sleeves, whom Mrs. James at first mistook for some of the relatives and was beginning to regale with her stories of the West Indies, pushed a few tables together so that we could all sit down. They then produced hundreds of little dishes of *tahina,* a sesame-seed concoction something like an American cheese dip, and *tabulli,* a salad of crushed wheat and chopped vegetables, while we ordered enough *kebbés* and *kanafas* to feed a regiment.

After we had been eating for some time and were beginning to feel drowsy, thinking all the while that we had never had so much food in all our lives, the relatives cried out,

144

"But you haven't eaten a thing!" and, despite our protests, piled our plates high all over again.

The only one who met with their approval was Helen, who ate so much she quite frightened them.

After lunch, which lasted just over two hours, we somehow managed to stand up and totter over to the car, which drove us straight to the St. George, where without another word we all promptly collapsed on our beds and slept the sleep of the dead.

When I awoke, the last rays of the sun were coming into the room. I went out onto the balcony and gazed at the beautiful Bay of St. George, where, so it is said, St. George slew the dragon. A few snow-white yachts still frolicked about and a motor boat trailing a water-skier buzzed in and out like a mischievous mosquito, leaving a white trail behind it. The mountains, parched at this time of year, but pink with the light of the setting sun, looked down serenely on happy Beirut.

We were to have dinner at Uncle Henri's house. Uncle Henri was one of my parents' numerous cousins. He was highly spoken of in Lebanon and, before going in for politics, he had been a successful lawyer. He was a big man, obviously fond of good living, and a connoisseur of rare books, old coins, rugs, and antiques. Though he was by no means lazy and indeed worked round the clock, he liked to be waited on hand and foot, and a barber, a pedicurist, and a masseur had, ever since I can remember, been known to attend him at the house. He spoke excellent French and was a brilliant conversationalist.

By the time we had dressed, the lights had begun to appear all over the mountains and we went down onto the terrace to wait for Uncle Henri's car and chauffeur, which were to take us up to Aley. Notwithstanding the fact that Beirut is supposed to be empty in the summer because everybody takes off for the mountains, the terrace was packed, and there was a large table of British naval officers. They immediately turned round to stare at Yvonne, which of course pleased Yvonne no end and Mother and Father not at all.

I could see Mother's busy little mind working.

"Come," she said quickly, fearing that one of the officers might be so bold as to come over and talk to Yvonne. "Let's wait inside. The car should be here any minute."

We did not wait long. Two minutes later, a big burly man with an enormous waxed mustache twirled upwards into two matchsticks came over and introduced himself as Uncle Henri's chauffeur.

We shot off, as though pursued by the FBI, through the tortuous, roller-coaster streets of Beirut, where old trams and brand-new cars rubbed shoulders and modern flats stood side by side with lattice-windowed old houses. How many eyes, I wondered, had peeped from behind those closed shutters onto the outside world of men. I remember Grandmother telling us how her own mother had never been outside the house in the whole of her life except to get married and be buried. We drove at break-neck speed, like everybody else, heedless of the most elementary rules of traffic regulations. We drove on the right, on the left, in the middle, on the pavement, and up streets clearly marked "No Entry." We overtook on curves and hills when we couldn't see what was coming—and just as well. I caught brief glimpses of alleyways and sooks lit by acetylene lamps, where, if one was not careful, one could easily pick up a bargain for twice the price one would pay in a good store downtown. Washing still hung from the balconies, and on them whole families sat looking down at the speeding cars honking like mad and filled with impatient people anxious to get up to the mountains.

It took us only a few minutes to get out of Beirut—though, with all the thrills which kept our hearts in our mouths, it seemed much longer—and soon we were on the road to Aley. The air all of a sudden was delightfully cool. Because it was dark, we could not see the rich red earth, or the crops, or the color of the sea, but we could smell the fragrance of pine trees. Hot and humid Beirut, now a mass of lights, lay behind us, and Aley appeared, a brightly lit shelf on the mountain, like some dazzling village in a fairy tale.

Uncle Henri's driver, telling us all the while how badly the other people drove, broke off the main road, tore up a very steep hill only wide enough for one car, and drew up in front of a house of rough gray stone snuggling in the midst of a small forest of pines.

The door was opened by a smart butler in a white jacket instead of the more customary sloppy female servant, and as he led us through the beautifully furnished living room, we saw straight ahead, framed by the large window leading onto the terrace where Uncle Henri and Aunt Louise sat waiting, the thousand and one lights of scintillating Beirut.

Uncle Henri and Aunt Louise came towards us, and again we were all kissing and talking at once. Aunt Louise was a very gracious woman with handsome features and a lively vivacious mind.

We were the first. The other guests had not yet arrived,

147

for people never arrive on time in Lebanon, no matter how Westernized they are. Mother asked Aunt Louise where her daughter Viviane was and Aunt Louise replied that she and Miss Shelley, the governess, had gone down to Beirut to fetch some British officers. "We met them last Christmas," explained Aunt Louise, "and their ships have just come in again."

"Really?" asked Mother, very surprised. "Oh, but I suppose," she added, "that they've been sick and are convalescing."

"What on earth gave you that idea?" Aunt Louise laughed.

"Do you mean to say that you and Henri allow Viviane to entertain healthy officers and to go out with them, too?" asked Mother incredulously.

"Why, yes," said Aunt Louise.

Mother looked worried.

"But Louise, in Alexandria the only girls who go out with soldiers are the Europeans, whose mentality is not the same as ours, and those who are . . . well, you know . . . not quite nice. Surely, if I were to allow my daughters to go out with officers, they would be referred to as not quite nice either."

Aunt Louise said, "Times are changing. What wasn't considered done yesterday will soon be looked upon as very proper and normal. Mark my words, times are changing. The more you forbid your daughters to go out, the more they will resort to deceit and do what they please anyway behind your back. I must say that I do prefer Viviane to invite her friends home, so that we can get to know them, too, and I have noticed that the officers she asks over are really very nice."

"Well, what about Miss Shelley?" Mother asked.

"We still have her," replied Aunt Louise, "but she is part of the family now, not a governess any more."

"Well, I don't know what to say," sighed poor Mother, "although I must admit that all the girls who seem to have eloped with the wrong people are the girls who were brought up very strictly."

There was the sound of gay voices and laughter and Viviane came in with Miss Shelley and five officers in tow. Viviane was pretty and you could tell she was very sure of herself. Her dress, which looked as though it had taken yards and yards of material, suited her beautifully, and she swished it elegantly as she walked. She pecked us lightly on the cheek and introduced us to the officers, who were standing around somewhat self-consciously.

Yvonne and I glanced at one another quickly, for we had realized the second they came in that the officers were the very same ones we had seen on the terrace of the St. George. Well, that was Fate. That wasn't Yvonne's doing. "You can delay the inevitable," Zeinap always said, "you cannot put it off forever."

Two of the officers, Colin and Peter, made a beeline for Yvonne, and Aunt Louise asked one called Ronnie, who had a neck like a giraffe's, if he wouldn't mind mixing us one of his specials. We all had one, even Mother, who never drank anything stronger than mulberry syrup.

The guests were beginning to trickle in. They looked plump, rested, and well fed. Drinks and hors d'oeuvres were passed round and it was eleven o'clock before we sat down to dinner at little tables. We helped ourselves from the lavish buffet and I wondered what those men fighting the war would say at the sight of such a spread.

Yvonne purred contentedly, her green eyes wide in amused anticipation as she gave the British Navy her "I'm so helpless" routine, which seemed to be working beautifully.

"Do have some of this," said the one called Peter.

"What is it?" asked Yvonne, batting her eyelids as though she had never seen vine leaves in all her life.

"What about some *foie gras?*" asked the one called Colin.

"Do you think I should?" murmured Yvonne, who loathed *foie gras.*

"Pigeons, Yvonne?" asked Peter.

"Prawns, Yvonne?" asked Colin.

And Yvonne continued to play the daily double and smile helplessly like the clever girl she was.

After coffee and liqueurs, some of the guests went inside to play bridge. The tables were removed as swiftly as they had appeared and we began to dance out on the terrace. It was a beautiful evening, and it was a new and not unpleasant experience to be able to talk to healthy officers.

Ronnie of the giraffe's neck bounced up to me and asked me for a dance.

"Your sister is very attractive," he said, as we waltzed to a fox trot. He was so tall that all I could see was a big brass button in the middle of my right eye; everything else was like a large white mountain. My poor arm was being pumped up and down like the old-fashioned gasoline pumps, and he was taking enormous steps, something like six to one.

I agreed with him that Yvonne was really very attractive.

"You're not a bit like her," said Ronnie. "I'm always

scared stiff of good-looking girls; that's why I feel so at ease with you," he added. I knew exactly what he meant. The convalescents were always telling me that I was a sport, a brick, and even that I reminded them of their sisters.

"You know," he asked, "who you remind me of?"

"Yes, your sister."

"I say, how jolly clever of you, old girl."

The music stopped and we walked over and leaned over the terrace railing. It was a balmy night and the breeze smelled of pine. The unrelenting voices of the crickets seemed to harmonize with the chatter of the guests, and Ronnie was a nice young man—average—even if I did remind him of his wretched sister. I wondered what Bill was doing now—but no, I wasn't going to think about Bill. The sky was littered with diamonds; indeed, the whole of Lebanon was one dazzling jewel.

Little by little the lights were going off in Beirut. My watch said three, and the party was breaking up. Uncle Henri's driver drove us down through the hushed streets in exactly the same leisurely way he had driven us up, and by a little after three-thirty we were back at the St. George.

As I got into bed, I couldn't help telling Yvonne, who was sharing the room with me, that she had been the belle of the ball. Yvonne sighed contentedly. "They were rather sweet," she said.

"Yes," I agreed, "but didn't you wish Karim was there?" I asked, sitting up on one elbow.

Yvonne stared at me as though she was realizing for the first time how stupid I really was. "Karim? Here? With all those handsome men around?" she cried. "What on earth for? Really, you do say the funniest things."

We saw a great deal of Viviane after that. Sometimes she'd take us to the beach. There are several beaches in and around Beirut, and although they don't compare with the beaches of Alexandria, they have the advantage of being only minutes away from the hills by car. One can come down from Aley or Bhamdoun in about twenty minutes and get back again in time for lunch. In the evenings, Viviane would take us to cocktail parties.

Before long, we moved up to Sofar. The Grand Hotel at Sofar was very chic. It was also on the Damascus Road and ideally situated if one wished to know who was driving where and with whom. Inside the hotel one played cards at all hours of the day or night, and outside, in the front garden where tables and chairs were spread out, one sat and sipped coffee. The men twiddled their amber beads and had their shoes polished by the shoeshine boys who carried elaborate brass boxes. Many smoked the narghile, the superior ones using their own special mouthpieces.

The hotel was full and we had many friends. Beatrice, her younger sister, and Miss Chalmers had also arrived from Alexandria after spending a few days in Jerusalem.

Sofar was very gay. Every evening we went to dinner dances in the garden of the hotel. There were always lots of people who came to Sofar from the neighboring villages, and there were usually a few tables of British and Free French Officers. To these battle-weary men, this tiny little country with its good-looking women, its nights scented with pine and perfume, and its huge banquets reminiscent of Roman orgies, must have appeared like some carefree paradise set in the middle of an angry world.

"Do you always live like this?" a Blues officer asked Viviane.

"I'm afraid we do," said Viviane. "Isn't it awful? I get so bored sometimes."

Viviane was not nearly as superficial as one would expect such a social person to be, and she took more than just a passing interest in politics, which was certainly unusual for a woman in the Middle East. She also taught French at one of the orphanages in Beirut. Viviane got on well with people, no matter who they were, and her circle of friends was quite fantastic, extending from the President himself to the gendarme at Djunieh. She knew everybody and everybody knew her.

While we drove around the country exploring Lebanon, Mother and Father remained for the most part at Sofar, and the relatives all came up in the afternoons, bringing with them huge baskets of fruit grown in their gardens. Sometimes they brought rich Lebanese desserts stuffed full of almonds or even homemade *kebbé*, and our room looked like a delicatessen. They were unbelievably kind and generous.

So we raced from one end of the country to the other, usually in groups of two or three cars, driving wherever the fancy took us. One day we'd go south along the coast, with its rich red earth and sub-tropical vegetation, in the direction of the ancient Phoenician city of Sidon (now Saida) . The next day we might explore the region of Tripoli and the Krak des Chevaliers, an old fortress built by the Crusaders.

Tripoli, a predominantly Moslem town, was the stronghold of Beatrice's family, who were Maronites. When we arrived there, Beatrice's numerous relatives all turned up to see us, down to the last cousin. We could not make out what they did for a living; they wore very casual clothes and did not seem to go to an office at all regularly, but they looked very happy and healthy. They really enjoyed life and had no desire to live anywhere else, and they spoke of Tripoli as though it was New York, Rome, and Paris all rolled into one. They treated us to an enormous lunch in the cool and pleasant garden of what was grandly known as Le Cercle. I gathered that the inhabitants of Tripoli spent most of their time at this little club, which badly needed a coat of paint, playing cards, twiddling their beads, and just watching people come and go. One of Beatrice's uncles, a pink-faced gentleman with twinkling blue eyes, told me that the Club was especially jolly at election time, when the candidates sometimes come in for a meal, sometimes for refuge. "I wouldn't be a candidate for anything," he said, "it's a very expensive business."

One weekend, a group of us went up to the Cedars. After negotiating endless hairpin bends and driving through scenery parched by the July sun, the dark blob up on the mountain that was the Cedars came into view.

The trees were once part of vast forests which covered the country in biblical days when Lebanon was the timberyard which supplied wood to the Phoenician coast and to neighboring Egypt. Now there are only about four hundred cedars left and, through the years, visitors have cut their names into the bark of the trees. On one of them is the name of Lamartine and his daughter Julia. The Lebanese are very proud of their Cedars, so much so in fact, that it has become the symbol appearing on the Lebanese flag.

We stayed at the hotel at the foot of the Cedars and slept in high old-fashioned beds, but the nice little maid who spoke very singsongy Lebanese slept on the floor in the

154

passage in her white daytime overall. We enjoyed the week-end immensely, and the air up at the Cedars, even in summer, is most invigorating.

The drive back to Sofar was to me perhaps the best part of all. That afternoon, as on most other late afternoons, the light was clear, the sky splashed with pink and purple light. We sped smoothly past Becharré, down the smooth gray ribbon, through a landscape of vines, shrubs, and quick-flowering plants, and the radio was playing a ringing over-ture familiar to us all but which we somehow couldn't place. Everyone was quiet, in contrast to the noisy exuberance with which we had set off—Viviane and the two British Guards she had brought along, a Lebanese boy called Pierre, who was driving, and Beatrice and myself.

Dishevelled by the wind, we finally drew up in front of the Grand Hotel at Sofar. We got out of the car, and as I walked into the lobby, British Guards to the right and to the left, the first person I saw sitting in a cloud of cigarette smoke was Bill. "Bill," I positively screamed, "what on earth are you doing here?"

Bill said "hi," he was now having his hundredth cigarette, but he said he'd spent a most enjoyable afternoon catching flies and tearing off their wings, and why shouldn't he come to Lebanon when everyone else was there, and what was I doing with all those not so sick men and who was the good-looking girl.

I was so eloquent that Bill had to repeat the questions all over again, but I finally managed to pull myself together and introduce him to Viviane and the Guards officers. When Viviane heard that Bill had spent the afternoon in the company of flies, she promptly invited him to the large dinner party Aunt Louise and Uncle Henri were having that night.

The last time I had seen Bill was shortly before he left on a trip to Italy. Over a game of Chinese checkers at the American Red Cross, I was bemoaning the fact that Father would not allow me to go into the world and get a job, or indeed do anything on my own.

"Concentrate on the game," said Bill. "Relax."

"Relax, relax," I said. "You don't understand how it feels to have all your ambitions knocked out of you, not to be able to do anything."

"You didn't see that move," Bill said. "Ha, ha, ha, now I've blocked you."

The man was maddening. Here I was trying to explain the problems of my very existence and all he said was "relax."

"But you don't understand; I really want a job," I said. "I want to feel I can stand on my own feet. Apart from anything else, one day I may be obliged to work for a living. Look at all those White Russians in Paris, earning a living as maids, doormen, and what have you. This sort of life here may not go on forever. And what then?" I asked him.

"It's your move," Bill said.

"Listen," I continued, "I have a friend who earns fifteen pounds a month teaching kindergarten. Her family do not approve of it, of course. But if she had been allowed to train in Europe, she could have earned far more and been able to make a living anywhere in the world. She would have been equipped for life."

"You're cheating," said Bill, looking straight at me with

those miserable blue eyes. "Anyway," he continued, "you won't need to be armed against life."

"Oh, no? And why not?" I asked.

"Because you're going to get married."

"Who says?"

"I do," said Bill, pleased with himself.

"Oh, really? And who do you have in mind, Colonel?" I asked, now quite sure that I knew the answer to that one.

"In mind? How should I know?" he replied.

Bill had somehow managed to find a room at the Grand Hotel, and I was very apprehensive as to what Mother would say when she saw him. As for Father, I hoped he wouldn't make an exception to the rule and recognize somebody for a change. However, by the time we left the hotel they had not yet bumped into one another, and I breathed a sigh of relief.

Halfway through the party at Aunt Louise's, Mother and Father, who had had dinner at some relatives' in Bhamdoum, suddenly appeared on the terrace. Father looked about him vaguely and went over to Uncle Henri, but Mother was heard to cry, very surprised, "Why, it's the American who plays the piano. What on earth are you doing here, Colonel?"

And Bill, instead of asking Mother for one good reason why he shouldn't come to the Lebanon when everyone else was there, or even regaling her with the bit about the flies' wings, turned on the charm and said how nice it was to see Mother and how lovely she looked in blue and how glad he was that the world was a small place. Mother, whose face had clouded at the sight of Bill, lapped up all the smooth talk like a pussycat and expressed her pleasure at seeing

Bill, and said that surely he would stay longer than five days in the Lebanon, and so on. I decided that when it came to shooting the breeze, there wasn't much to choose between an American and a Lebanese.

Helen, who spoke little but still too much, then came up with some pimply girl in her early teens and said nonchalantly, "Odette, this is Bill Carol, my sister's lover."

The proceedings were further enlivened by the arrival of a couple I had never seen before, but who were obviously not Lebanese. The man reminded me of a little black spider, but the woman, whose décolleté was somewhere round her knees, caused something of a stir. Aunt Louise's well-trained butler was so moved that he shot straight off the steps of the terrace into some bushes with his tray of drinks. The women, who had been gossiping in a corner, jumped up in a body to protect their husbands from the menace, and the dancing suddenly stopped.

"Hullo . . . o," sighed the voluptuous creature in the kind of breathless voice which suggested she had run up all the way from Beirut. She put out her hand langorously and all the men collapsed over it.

"I'm so glad you could come tonight, Lala," said Uncle Henri, patting her shoulder unnecessarily.

"Han—ri, of course I come to see you," she said, batting her eyelids. "As my third husband said to me—smile, Micha, smile," she pinched his cheek, "he said, I am very poor, so we'll just have a bottle of champagne at the St. George and then we'll go to Han—ri and Louise."

"Who is she?" I whispered to Viviane.

"She says she's Rumanian," Viviane whispered back. "She

158

just turned up in the Lebanon one day in a yacht, with a man she said was her third husband, and a lot of jewelry."

"I just luff men," Lala was saying. "Men and a little bit money and, of course, my little Micha here. Smile, Micha, smile. Isn't he sweet?" she asked.

Micha showed his teeth. Viviane said, "You know, the third husband was really good-looking, sort of Hollywood, but penniless. Lala told Mother confidentially that when she first saw Micha she thought he was hideous, but she didn't think he looked quite so bad when she discovered he was rolling in money and had half a dozen titles."

The party went off very well, with Lala getting more and more breathless and trying to find out if any of the men present were wealthier than her Micha. We did not get home until the early hours of the morning, absolutely exhausted, especially after our jaunt to the Cedars. To my surprise, neither Mother nor Father mentioned Bill, and I wondered whether Aunt Louise had had anything to do with it. Nor did they say anything when he accompanied us on all our excursions for the five days he remained in the Lebanon.

Bill liked Lebanon and the friendly, voluble Lebanese. Viviane organized his program so that he could get to see as much of the country as was possible in the five days. We visited Byblos, from which the Bible got its name. To get there, we crossed the Dog River where the various conquerors—Pharaohs, Assyrians, Greek, French, and British—have carved inscriptions on the rocks. Then we continued along the road through the town of Djunieh with its picturesque fishing harbor and orange groves. The houses were of rough gray stone and bright garments hung from the

159

windows to dry. The earth was of that rich red color which is so often seen in Lebanon, but the coast was rugged rock and shingles. Byblos itself is very tiny and the chief attraction of the place is its castle overlooking the sea. A guide showed us around, explaining that Byblos was once the great commercial and religious center of the Phoenician coast. Like the other Phoenician cities, Byblos fell to the various conquerors, including Alexander the Great, Pompey, Saladin, and the Crusaders, and its history, full of myths and legends, is a colorful one.

The next day, we took Bill to Baalbeck, and we stopped to have lunch at Zahlé on the way.

Zahlé is synonymous with food—and more especially grilled chicken. It is very green and wooded and it is cut in two by a waterfall pouring down over jagged rocks, but one goes there just to eat. We sat on benches at crude wooden tables with checkered tablecloths, practically on the stream itself. The talkative Lebanese waiter in shirt sleeves brought us a mass of little dishes into which we dipped with paper-thin bread. Then came the tender grilled chicken, which we ate with our fingers and which we washed down with ice-cold beer. And we scooped jugfuls of water from the stream—said to be very healthful—without so much as moving from the table. After washing our hands at the open-air row of little basins provided for the guests, we slumped back on our benches and sipped coffee, and it was at this precise moment that the inevitable photographer appeared and snapped us for posterity.

We did not get to Baalbeck until well after four, and the two hours we spent there were enough to give Bill only the vaguest idea of the splendor of Baalbeck. By the light of the setting sun, we wandered through the various courts littered with fragments of large stones and explored the Roman temples of Jupiter and Bacchus, gazing in awe at their high colonnades ornamented with friezes, until it was too dark to see. Bill took countless pictures and was not satisfied until, like a typical American, he had obtained all the statistical details of every arch, column, and stone he came across.

The five days we spent showing Bill the Lebanon made me see the country with new eyes, not merely as a rich playground in which to enjoy oneself but as a mosaic of past civilizations—Ancient Egyptian, Roman, Greek, Phoenician, Crusader, French—all of which have left some important vestige.

The day before he left, Bill asked if I would help him bargain-hunt for a gift for his sister. Though Mother did not approve of my going down to Beirut alone with Bill unchaperoned, she finally allowed me to do so. We went down in a service taxi which screeched to a stop outside the Grand Hotel, and I felt very wicked and depraved as all the people sitting in the garden stared at me disapprovingly, wondering how George and Marie permitted their daughter to carry on like that.

Bill was quite convinced that no one would take him for an American since he wasn't wearing his general's jacket with the wings and the row of ribbons.

"I'm really incognito." He winked, very pleased with himself, like a naughty little schoolboy who is about to pull off a gag, quite oblivious of his crew cut, his green Polaroid glasses, and especially of the way he walked, that dislocated walk which I have only seen in those who come from the other side of the Atlantic.

161

We got out at Bab Idriss, and as we walked towards the sook, I briefed Bill to keep his mouth shut and not utter a single word, for the price would treble if the salesman suspected he was one of those rich Americans.

"But we're not rich," protested Bill, "it's a fallacy."

"Nevertheless," I insisted, "just let me do the talking and I'll get you a real bargain."

Down the narrow sook we went, with all the little stores on either side hung with leather bags, amber beads, and ivory, and the salesmen waiting outside them beckoning and inviting us just to come in and look around. We went inside some dark little place which was delightfully cool after the hot sun. There were brocades everywhere and the dusty glass cases were brimful of old jewelry and oriental odds and ends. Drinking cups of Turkish coffee, we sat comfortably on a Bokhara-covered sofa while the salesman outdid himself in an effort to sell us everything he had in the store. My attention was suddenly arrested by a bracelet inlaid with different colored stones which Bill and I agreed was just the thing we were looking for.

"You can tell it's typically Phoenician," I said, feeling very superior. "It must be a million B.C. if it's a day." And Bill, who was forbidden to speak, nodded wisely, as though to say, "Phoenician, of course. Well, go ahead. I leave it to you."

So the salesman and I got down to brass tacks and the haggling started and went on for hours. In the end, practically in tears, the man pushed the bracelet towards me whining that I was the hardest bargainer he had ever seen and that I was literally taking the bread out of his mouth. I

162

did not believe a word of it, but nevertheless, we returned to Sofar well pleased with ourselves.

When Bill unwrapped the bracelet to admire the gift that looked so typically Phoenician, there it was, engraved in very small letters—"Made in Japan."

11

Just Name It—Cairo Has It

"Quite," the soldier who came to Cairo on leave from the desert would say. "If you mean flies, bugs, dust, heat, fountain pens which don't work, and cheap cabarets, then Cairo has it and Cairo probably has more of it than any other city in the world." On the basis of his short leave in Cairo, he made up his mind that the whole of Egypt was a land of squalor and disease where the native population was out to cheat him. It was small comfort to him to be told, after his wallet had been spirited away, that the cause lay in incredible poverty.

I liked Cairo, which was very un-Alexandrian of me. An Alexandrian grumbles for about ten days before he has to go up there that he has some business to attend to in Cairo. He takes the Pullman train to the capital, rushes about during the hottest hours, and tears back to Alex the same evening, moaning and groaning about the heat, the dirt, the flies, and the ministries. Or, over Christmas, perhaps, he spends a week at Mena House sitting with his back to the Pyramids and talking to other Alexandrians about, of course, Alexandria.

To me, Cairo was such a change after Alexandria. It was a city—in fact, the largest in Africa—gay, cosmopolitan, sophisticated, with fine new buildings and scores of restaurants, up-to-date cinemas and stores, an opera house, wide streets and large squares. It was East and West at once. In no time at all, you could plunge into narrow winding lanes where houses still had tiny grilled windows for the women of the harem, and the men prayed in the middle of the street outside the mosques. Cairo was a melting pot of old and new. It was the headquarters of the British Army, the temporary home of exiled governments, the scene of top-level conferences, where camels swayed alongside Cadillacs and modern bridges spanned the ancient Nile.

The Nile, which after its birth in the depths of Africa flows through miles and miles of barren desert until at Cairo it fans out into a fertile green triangle populated by some twenty million inhabitants, meant different things to different people. To the well to do, it was a cool breeze and a beautiful view from a luxury apartment at Zamalek and perhaps a houseboat at Dokki. But a few hundred yards away, at Roda, where it is said Pharaoh's daughter found Moses in the bulrushes, women in black bathed their naked children, scrubbed their big copper pans, and filled their earthenware jugs with the same brown water.

Cairo was a bustling, colorful city. On Kasr-el-Nil Street, smart women tripped out of flashy American cars to do their shopping, and came out again followed by their chauffeurs carrying the parcels. On the pavement, the crowd was a motley one. Well-dressed people in European clothes rubbed shoulders with women in black *milayas,* the hems of gawdy flowered prints peeping at the ankles. Sunburned Tommies just back from the desert, the backs of their necks very red, saluted officers dripping gold braid and medals, and men sold fizzy lemonade on street corners.

And of course, there was Shepheard's.

Shepheard's was not a beautiful place but it had a certain something. It was large and it was old, with potted palms in the corners, brass bedsteads in the bedrooms, pillars and weird lotus designs all over the place. In the lounge lit by feeble colored lights, there were divans, musharabia screens, and low coffee tables adorned with mother-of-pearl. The hotel was always crowded. This was the place you'd meet the brigadier you did not want to meet, and the aunt who had never been outside Blackpool, and this was the place, too, where you'd get an eyeful of showy but beautiful Levantines escorted by fat, balding husbands.

In November, my favorite month of all in Egypt, I went up to Cairo to spend ten days with Aunt Lolotte and Uncle Victor. Not only was Aunt Lolotte my favorite aunt, but it was also, so I thought, a cunning way of seeing Bill.

I took the Pullman train from Sidi-Gaber station. The platform contained the usual handful of prosperous people and the mass of barefooted Arabs, loaded with bundles, baskets, and children, who could climb into the third-class compartment—through the window, more likely than not. In the middle of the platform were first- and second-class passengers—Italian families who sounded as though they were rehearsing Verdi, a couple of Catholic priests in brown robes and sandals, Egyptian students spouting fire and brimstone, and a group of British soldiers patiently sitting on their packs having a shoeshine.

A gong announced the approach of the train and, with

many admonitions from Mother to behave like a lady at my aunt's, I boarded the Pullman. Like some monster with an insatiable appetite, it swallowed practically everyone on the platform, and, having had its fill, moved off slowly. "Would Her Excellency the Madam like some coffee?" asked the suffragi, a big podgy man with skin the color of the ace of spades and two large scars on his cheeks. Her Excellency the Madam said she'd like a coffee, and presently he brought it along with a glass of water.

It was most pleasant to be sitting in the deep, comfortable armchair with a table in front of me, sipping coffee and watching the landscape go by. The earth on either side was green and brown, rich with crops and dotted wth eucalyptus, palms, and banana trees. Willows stooped towards the muddy little canal which escorted the tracks. Fellaheen, too busy to look at the passing train, bent over in their fields of cotton—that cotton which was Egypt's main source of wealth and which one saw packed in bales, stacked on lorries and feluccas and trains on its way to world markets. Every now and then we passed a cluster of mud huts, shapeless, like the mud pies children make at the seaside. In these, with their families and animals, the fellaheen lived. A mosque was never far away.

The suffragi appeared with the menu for lunch. There was hors d'oeuvres, spaghetti with bolognaise sauce, roast veal with vegetable, salad, cheese, fruit, and coffee. All for twenty-five piastres. It came along quickly and it was hot and good, and as the train slowed down because of repairs on the tracks, I glanced out the window and saw workmen in ragged galabias and scarves round their heads sitting

167

on the ground sharing a meal of beans and dark Arabic bread.

Under the warm winter sun with fluffy white clouds floating by, very brown fellaheen ploughed the land with the help of their oxen, and a water buffalo plodded resignedly round and round, turning the water wheel. The train rattled over Benha Bridge and I caught a quick glimpse of tall, graceful feluccas and a mass of women in black doing their laundry on the banks of the Nile. Off the bridge now and speeding towards Cairo, only thirty minutes away. How time had flown! Women walked on the path alongside the train balancing heavy earthenware jugs on their heads. Barefooted, with silver bracelets round the ankles, they held themselves straight and their arms swung easily. I had seen them walk that way all my life—in fact I had tried to imitate them without much success—but it was Mrs. James who first pointed out to me the inborn grace of their movements.

The attendant came in now to take my suitcase off the rack. The train whistled past slummy dwellings which looked as though they wouldn't survive someone blowing on them, let alone an earthquake, and we pulled in at Cairo station. It was noisy and crowded as usual, with porters, soldiers, policemen, women with babies—all coming and going at once. Aunt Lolotte's tall, smart Sudanese driver Mohamed suddenly appeared at my elbow and grabbed my suitcase from an indignant porter, and we made towards the car.

We drove to Aunt Lolotte's villa in Zamalek and, as I had expected, the house was full of people. It always was, for Aunt Lolotte belonged to every committee, every organization in town, hobnobbed with all the ambassadors and ministers, was invited to all the cocktail parties, dinner parties, garden parties, and balls, and was one of the leading lights of Cairo society. Consequently, if people were not coming to her house for a committee meeting, they were coming to sell her tickets for some charity, or to play bridge or to take her shopping, or even just to ask her advice, and because she was so softhearted, she never refused anyone anything.

Aunt Lolotte greeted me with outstretched arms. "But where on earth have you been?" she cried. "You're the same color as Mohamed—no, darker, so help me." I tried to explain that I still spent most of my time at Sidi-Bishr Beach, but she wasn't listening. She was telling me that I was to consider this my home and that I could ask anyone I liked over for a drink or dinner, "as many friends as you wish, Darling, and if you need anything, just ring for Emilia."

Aunt Lolotte was bubbling over. She always was. "Before I forget, Dear," she said, "there's a big ball on tonight, and of course, you are coming along with us. Your Uncle Victor and I have invited Mr. Kirk, *le Ministre Plénipotentiaire des Etats Unis,* and also the British Ambassador—oh no, he's ill, but his wife is coming—and let me see, oh yes, an Indian major who speaks beautiful English, the French Consul from Port Said, some Lebanese friends, and an air commodore and his wife. They're all coming to drinks first. There should be a good floor show and Tahia Carioca is going to dance."

All this Aunt Lolotte explained without taking a breath, and she was very pleased when I said that I would just love to come, for she was very distressed that her only daughter hated social life as much as she loved it. "And Darling," she added, "ask anyone you like along tonight. Haven't you got a friend or two in Cairo you'd like to have come along?"

I thought it over very carefully for exactly half a second

and then called Bill. He turned up very smartly at eight, which actually wasn't such a smart thing to do because Aunt Lolotte was not ready. The trouble with Aunt Lolotte was that she had nothing to wear and was taking three hours to put it on, as usual.

Finally we were ready, and Aunt Lolotte, very smart in a pale gray brocade dress, and I were descending the marble staircase. Bill was waiting in the brightly lit salon looking as devastating as he always did in his uniform. Aunt Lolotte greeted him effusively. She was so happy to meet him. She just loved Americans and he wasn't to worry about being a fish out of water because there was going to be another American there as well, a charming man. When Bill beamed and asked who it was, Aunt Lolotte said it was the American *Ministre Plénipotentiaire,* whereupon Bill said "Oh."

It was one of the things I liked about her that she knew how to make a person feel at ease. She had a fund of stories, and she started to tell us about her visit to the States just before the war. "I got into a cab," she said, "on my first day in New York, and, not knowing how much to tip the driver, I told him quite frankly, 'This is my first visit to New York and I don't know how much I should give you. Will this be enough?' " Aunt Lolotte laughed. "The fare was sixty cents and I was handing him a dollar, but I had heard that New York cab drivers expected a large tip. Well," continued Aunt Lolotte, "the man said, yeah, he figured it would just do, and then he asked me: 'Say, Lady, where you from?' I told him I came from Cairo. 'Cairo? Gee, that's a nice place,' the cab driver replied. 'You've been there?' I asked, surprised. 'Oh, sure,' said the driver, 'Cairo, Illinois— very nice place, very nice place indeed.' "

The guests now arrived, and Aunt Lolotte's suffragis, in white gloves and splendid royal blue and gold outfits, passed round trays of drinks and hors d'oeuvres. Everyone chatted easily about the latest reception, the progress of the war, how to make tahina, and guess who they saw at Shepheard's. As Aunt Lolotte had said, the American Minister was a charming man, and he and Bill exchanged several hilarious stories which nobody else quite understood.

Towards ten-thirty we got into the cars and proceeded to the ball, which lasted until dawn. I can still see, as though it were yesterday, the chic, beautifully dressed women in costly furs and jewels, the royalty, pashas, and diplomats, the Guards with their pink aristocratic faces and tapering trousers, the fat prosperous businessmen dancing and laughing, and the Heidsieck in the buckets of ice. I haven't forgotten the extravagant spectacle of the hundreds of fleet-footed suffragis carrying high on one hand large silver dishes groaning with turkeys and enormous fish, while outside, barefooted kids waited by the chromium plated cars to receive half a piastre. "There are so many beggars," people said, "what can one do? We all have our charity organizations to support." And it was true. Later on in the evening, we adjourned to the cabaret tent—a bright tent of kaleidoscope colors—to watch Tahia Carioca unleash tumultuous applause with her inimitable and provocative belly-dancing. The whole evening has remained in my memory as a glittering page from a fairy-tale world which has ceased to exist.

Another memory also belongs to the fabulous war days. This was during another visit to Cairo. It was the middle of August and Aunt Lolotte was taking me to a large party on board a houseboat moored at Dokki. "Who says Cairo isn't

171

gay in the summer?" she said. As we approached the glittering houseboat, strains of music reached our ears and women in evening dress could be seen moving about the ship while suffragis weaved in and out. And then we got out of the car and I saw something I have never forgotten, though it did not particularly shock me at the time. Because it was August and the Nile was high, the gangway which the guests had to walk on to get to the boat rested on the shoulders of a dozen or so ragged-looking men. Clad in their usual filthy galabias, the ends of which they had grabbed between their teeth, they stood in the slush while the guests, women in expensive gowns and men in spotless white sharkskin jackets, tripped lightheartedly onto the boat.

I went shopping with Aunt Lolotte every morning of the ten days I spent in Cairo. Aunt Lolotte did not patronize the large stores, only the little shops, and we never got out of the car, for the business was always conducted through the open window. Perhaps this is where the idea of the drive-ins originated. "I know of a wonderful little man who makes lampshades," she'd say in an undertone, as though she was divulging a state secret, or "a wonderful little man who makes handbags of fly covers for cakes; in fact, he is the one who makes them for the large stores." And Osta Mohamed, the chauffeur, would drive us to some narrow little side street crawling with wonderful little men who worked outside dark holes-in-the-ground and even in the middle of the street, like Maalim Abou Bakr the carpenter, and turned out good inexpensive workmanship.

Aunt Lolotte would roll down the window and old Maalim Abou Bakr, who had made furniture for Aunt Lolotte's family for years, would smile and tell her that the day was so much brighter now that she had come. He'd say to the dark-eyed little boy standing by his side, "Go quickly and fetch a coffee for the lady." Aunt Lolotte, who drank around a dozen coffees a day, would continue to sit in the car, sipping it slowly, taking her time, asking questions about Maalim Abou Bakr's health and about his eldest son—he had eleven children not counting those who had died—who did not want to be a carpenter but was ambitious to work in an office. Maalim Abou Bakr would say "*Maalish, maalish*—never mind—such is the will of Allah," and then he'd show Aunt Lolotte the tea trolley he was making for her just like the one in the English magazine.

Aunt Lolotte drove away well pleased with her shopping, and she would turn to me and whisper, "You must never give any of those addresses away to anyone, not anyone, you understand." But when, an hour later, a friend admired her handbag or her hand-embroidered tablecloth, she'd put her hand across her mouth and say, "If you promise not to tell anyone, I'll give you the address of the little man who made it for me," for Aunt Lolotte was good at lots of things, but not at keeping secrets.

We'd wind up the morning by meeting some of Aunt Lolotte's friends for an apéritif at Groppi's. In its little garden, baby-faced lieutenants and three-star generals drank Tom Collinses beside olive-skinned Syrians and swarthy men in fezzes sipping coffee noisily. I was never bored at Groppi's.

As always in the wintertime, day followed day in unbroken sunshine and cloudless skies. The air was dry and healthy and there was almost no rain. When rain does come in Egypt, though, it is usually in the form of a downpour. In the sum-

173

mer Cairo is very warm, with temperatures in the 90's, sometimes more, and in August, when the Nile rises, it is very
humid as well; but from October to about April, the weather
is really beautiful.

Bill managed to get away from Payne Field most afternoons, and sometimes he played golf at the Gezira Sporting
Club, a truly beautiful club with acres of green fields, and I'd
totter behind him trying to keep up with his enormous strides,
trailing him round the course, in spite of my Western ideas
looking for all the world like an Eastern slave, quite forgetful
of the fact that I hated to walk and hadn't a clue as to what
the game was all about anyway. Strangely enough Bill, who
was usually as good-tempered as a toy teddy bear, would act
very peculiarly and look right through me, even though it
had been his idea that I should accompany him. He teed off
and sliced and went down on all fours with his eye to the
ground to measure something which never made any difference in the end, and putted and missed and hooked and got
mad and pleased and mad again all over a wretched little ball
which half the time I could never see anyway, though I naturally pretended that I could. I'd find it difficult to understand what Bill's fury was all about. "Relax," I'd venture to
say when Bill was beginning to act like a Karamazov, and a
fuming Bill would turn round and just glare at me through
those half-shut eyes of his, and the grinning, barefooted caddies who were always full of praise for the way the Captain
handled his clubs would tell him over and over again that he
played "berry good, berry well," because they were smart, not
like me, and that was precisely what the captain overpaid
them to hear.

Afterwards, we'd have tea in the clubhouse, crowded with

174

attractive well-dressed women, contented pashas, and polo-playing British officers with ginger mustaches. Bill would then become very pleasant and chatty, and he'd elaborate not only on the game he had just played, analyzing each stroke, but on every ball he'd ever hit since he was ten years old. The golf bug is a miserable thing, especially for those who have not been bitten.

Bill was fond of saying that one could buy anything on a Cairo street. "Just name it, Cairo has it," he liked to joke. Early one evening, we were sitting on the balcony of Shepheard's having a drink, when something happened which proved how right he was. One of the innumerable salesmen who patronized Shepheard's came up to our table and proceeded to exhibit his merchandise all over the place.

"Go away," I said to him in Arabic, just to show him that I was a local product and that he was wasting his time.

"I'm not talking to you," he replied, "I'm talking to the Captain. Look, Captain, beautiful ivory camel. Only one bound." (There is no P in Arabic.) "Berry good, berry nice." (There is no V either, but there are two S's, two D's, two H's, a "kha," and several things which can quite easily bring up your tonsils.)

"One pound for that?" Bill cried.

"*Maalish*, for you, Captain, seventy biastres," the man said. Bill didn't answer.

"Fifty," said the salesman.

"Thirty biastres. O.K., twenty biastres, for you, Captain." Bill still didn't answer.

"Fifteen biastres for you, Captain," the man said.

"That's a real good price," Bill said, "but I really don't want a camel. What would I do with a camel?"

175

The man was more persistent than a fly. "O.K. What you want? I got everything," he said. "You want jewel, statue of Sphinx? Brocade?" Then he lowered his voice and leaned towards Bill. "You want a girl? Italian, Greek, French? Berry berry nice and clean; pink outside, pink inside. Only five bounds."

"Well," Bill said, "that sure sounds fascinating, but no, thank you. Wait a minute, though, tell you what I do need. I need a wardrobe to keep my clothes in. You get me one and I'll give you five bounds."

The salesman gathered his leather wallets, sunglasses, fly whisks, ivory bric-a-brac, and brocades and made off without a word. Bill and I roared with laughter and ordered another drink. "I think you've really offended him," I said.

Half an hour had barely gone by when the man reappeared.

"Where you want your wardrobe, Captain?" he asked. On the pavement a couple of yards from where we sat, a crony stood waiting doubled up in two. Strapped to his back was an enormous brown cupboard.

There was much to do and see in Cairo and Aunt Lolotte allowed me to come and go as I pleased.

"Enjoy yourself, Darling," she'd say. "To my knowledge one lives but once, but of course, do remember to be a lady." Like all the tourists, Bill and I went sight-seeing, exploring the Pyramids and the Sphinx, where we were pestered by guides and camel men, and having tea in the garden at Mena House. We visited the Azhar—a mosque and university combined and the chief theological seminary in the Islamic world—and we went shopping in the Khan-el-Khalil Bazaar. There we spent hours exploring the little shops which overflowed with exquisite merchandise—ivory, amber, jewelry and trinkets, leather hassocks, and camel saddles—and we watched the craftsmen tapping the silver filigree threads into the copper trays and cigarette boxes. In some cool little store lit with a colorful bronze Musky lantern, we rested and sipped a Turkish coffee as the salesman unfurled yards and yards of silk and brocades, draping them about him to show them off. We felt like buying the whole lot.

I discovered that Bill knew far more about Egypt and its history than I did. From the ancient monuments which the dry, rainless weather has helped preserve in good condition, and the museums rich with antiquities which Bill wanted to visit again and again, we followed the history of Egypt through the various epochs, Pharaonic, Greek, Roman, Christian, and Islamic. I learned how as far back as three thousand years before the birth of Christ, the Egyptians had attained a high degree of civilization with commerce, building, and writing. Mummies especially fascinated us, and in the Museum near the Kasr-el-Nil Bridge, where one can see the fabulous treasures of the Tut-Ankh-Amen collection discovered by Howard Carter, we spent hours looking at them.

It was in this manner and in the company of an American that, for the first time, I learned something of the splendor of Ancient Egypt, which I had not so much as heard mentioned at either of the two schools I had attended because we were so busy learning about the battles of Hastings and Waterloo and rattling off by heart long lists of all the French *départements* and *sous-préfectures*. Now, with Bill, I learned how the Ancient Egyptians believed in life after death as long as the body could be preserved, and how after removing the viscera and filling the cavity with spices and resin, they bound up the body in linen—very fine linen for kings—and placed

177

it in a coffin which they deposited in the tomb. On the walls and ceiling of the tomb they painted pictures and wrote inscriptions in beautiful hieroglyphs, and they placed in the tomb all the things they thought the person would need in the next life.

On my last day in Cairo, we rode in Bill's jeep through the streets of the city and to the Citadel by the Mokattam Hills. In the courtyard, a few elderly Egyptians were performing their ablutions before entering to pray in this most famous of Cairo mosques, built by Saleh-el-Din in the twelfth century. We took off our shoes and put on special canvas slippers and, with a guide, we went round silently, awed by the magnificence of the place. The floors were covered with rugs, the walls were of alabaster and mosaic with elaborate inscriptions in Arabic of the names of the Prophet's followers. From the high cupola, immense chandeliers made little clinking glass sounds and hundreds of round bulbs hung down on rods, bathing the mosque in a golden light.

It had been chilly inside, and when we came out, we stood for a moment warming ourselves in the late afternoon sun as we looked down onto the conglomeration of flat-roofed dwellings, little back gardens, graceful minarets, slums, tombs, churches, and modern advertisements that was Cairo. The Pyramids of Giza, pale and dusty in the distance, seemed not quite real, and the island of Gezira, with its smart apartment houses and villas and its Sporting Club, was like a green oasis in the midst of the sand-colored city.

Bill lit one of his beloved Camels, blew out a cloud of smoke, and then said, "What do you say we get married in May? It's a good season for fishing."

This seemed to me such an excellent reason that, throwing

to the winds everything that had ever been instilled into me about Lebanese husbands for Lebanese girls, and blissfully forgetful of the fact that I would have to face the family, I agreed with unladylike alacrity that no season could be better.

What a to-do there was.

Bill was to go to Father's office and get his consent. "I'm not the least bit worried," were Bill's famous last words as he set off.

Ha! He was so unworried at the thought of tackling Father that he did not even make it to the elevator of Father's building.

A few days later, we met secretly at one of the less distinguished cafés in the neighborhood of Ramleh Station. We figured that we would be less likely to be seen in such dubious surroundings. So off Bill went on his second assignment to Father's office and I sat awaiting his return while half a dozen undistinguished-looking people occasionally turned round to stare.

To compose myself, I ordered coffee, Coca-Cola, and a fizzy lemonade, and at one point, the Greek who owned the place came over to chat. Greeks are friendly, especially those who own cafés.

He just wanted to tell me that he thought my captain friend was "very, very nice," and, he added, in tones which implied that he and Bill had been buddies at school together, "very, very intelligent."

He also wanted to know if I was making good money.

"Oh, no," I said, "I don't do anything for money." That pleased him.

"For fun, eh?" he beamed. "Excellent, excellent. Maybe

179

you accept little gifts, no? But later, you take money, yes?" He removed the soggy toothpick he had been chewing.

"What business are your Mama and Papa in?" he asked matily.

"I beg your pardon?"

"What they do now?" he asked.

I wanted to tell him that I didn't know what they do now, but that I was a little apprehensive about what they do later.

At last, Bill appeared. He had been gone for over two hours. His face dripped with perspiration. He looked beaten, as though he'd fought Rommel singlehanded.

"What happened?" I asked.

Bill slumped into a chair. "He said no. Honestly, there wasn't one single argument I put forward that he didn't demolish," Bill said.

"Really, Bill, I didn't expect anything different," I said.

"Relax," said Bill. "The course of true love never did run smooth. It'll just take us a little longer, that's all. But it had better not be too long."

"Well, I'd better run, or I'll be late for lunch."

At the best of times, there was no question of his coming home to lunch unless he was formally asked by Mother and Father, and that appeared to be definitely out now. I said good-bye and drove back alone.

When I reached home, the house was in an uproar. The glad tidings had arrived before I had. Mother was standing at the top of the stairs and she was very upset. Mother never raised her voice. She didn't have to. She could get a better effect by just weeping gently, steadily, like good English drizzle.

180

"I'm so upset, I can hardly say a word," she said. Mother was not always very accurate.

"How could you, how could you, encouraging a *man* like that." (I wondered what specie I was supposed to encourage.) "You, the eldest, the supposedly sensible one. Oh, after all we tried to teach you, the upbringing we gave you. A *soldier.* How can you marry a *soldier?* Well, all right, a flyer then. It is unthinkable. Why, the washerwoman's daughter married a soldier. Do you want to be bracketed with the washerwoman? Just look at what happened to poor Beatrice. Thank heavens that was stopped in time. No, I can't go on. My heart is broken."

So Mother went on. "What do you know about this soldier? What kind of family does he come from? What diseases do they have? Maybe they have idiots in the family—I wouldn't be surprised. Who knows? Maybe he himself has some dreadful disease?"

"Mother, if he had some dreadful disease, he wouldn't be in the Air Force."

"Don't answer back. I'm your mother," said Mother brightly, "and I know what is best for you. Perhaps I have only myself to blame, convincing your father that there was no harm in your going to the hospitals and the Red Cross." She dabbed her lovely blue eyes, which were as red as a bunny's from crying.

"Anyway," said Mother, "what's the hurry? Why don't you both wait a couple of years before getting married?"

"Because, Mother, Bill has to leave and the States isn't exactly next door," I said.

"Oh, dear," said Mother, suddenly thinking of something

181

new and terrible, "don't tell me that it's because you've done—you've done something you shouldn't have!"

"Mother," I howled, "do I look as though I'd know how to do anything I shouldn't have?"

Whereupon Father came in. He looked right through me and didn't say a word. I preferred it when he shouted. A heavy silence—the eve-of-battle kind—descended upon the house and we all went to have lunch. Our most glorious battles were often fought at lunch.

I was really upset and couldn't even look at my plate, but good old Helen just ate. "She'll probably marry a pig," I thought unkindly. "Make a good match, too. That girl hasn't got a nerve in her body, just food." Every now and again Yvonne glanced at me sympathetically. Mrs. James made a couple of remarks about the poor Duke of Windsor and how he had to give up everything for that dreadful American woman. Apparently, the Duke's case and mine were similar. But no one was amused. It occurred to me that in many other countries, such a proposal of marriage might have been an occasion for rejoicing. I had seen movies and read books in which a girl's parents prayed that she should marry a nice American G.I.

Suddenly, Father threw down the gauntlet in the form of his napkin and brought his fist down on the table with a terrifying thump. "Who does this monkey in uniform think he is, I'd like to know? How does he think he can support a wife and children, a kid like that? The gall, the cheek of it! Why, I didn't get married until I was well-established in business and had made a name for myself."

The war drums were beating inside me. I'd never been so angry in my life. "I don't care about marrying somebody who

182

is well-established in business," I shouted back. "I'm not interested in marrying a bank."

"A bank? A bank? How dare you? Where would you be if it weren't for your Father, who provides you with everything? Where would you be, all of you?" Father glared.

"Hush, Dear," said Mother pathetically, tugging at his sleeve. "She doesn't mean what she is saying."

"Yes, I mean it," I cried. "I want to live my own life for a change. Everyone is entitled to that. People fight wars over it," I said dramatically, "and I'm going to marry whom I jolly well please." But in truth, at this point, I wasn't convinced of this myself.

"Don't shout at your Father," said Mother, "he knows what's best for you. You don't have to marry anybody right now."

"Have you stopped to consider," said Father, more quietly, "what it would be like, living in America, cooking and cleaning and living on his salary? Why, you'd be worse off than one of the servants. You've never even washed a pair of stockings in your life."

"I've never had to," I said, boiling with rage.

"You could never keep house without servants," Father cried.

"How do I know what I'm capable of doing when I've never been allowed to try anything?" I replied hotly.

"The ingratitude!" roared Father. "What better life could you possibly hope for than the one right here, among your own kind of people?"

"Everything you've ever wanted you've always had," said Mother sadly. "You mean you want to throw everything away and go and live in some strange foreign country?"

183

"I can't understand your attitude," cried Father. "I should have thought that a Father's word was law."

It was my turn to bring my fist down onto the table. I got up and stalked out. I went upstairs and locked myself in my room. I knew that if they persisted in their attitude there was nothing I could do. I couldn't just go off like that. Or could I?

There was a knock on the door.

"Go away, you medieval monsters," I howled. On looking back, I think I must have been demented.

"Open up, my precious lamb, it's Maha." I opened the door six inches and said suspiciously, "Well, what do you want?"

"I've brought you some food," she said. I told her to go to hell.

"Never mind, never mind," she cooed. "No matter what happens, you must eat." Food, clothes, the common everyday things that you could touch and smell—these Maha understood.

"I have an idea," said the good simple soul. "If you want to get married, why don't you marry a Lebanese? Is there anything to beat a nice Lebanese husband? And then you know what? Maha will come and take care of the babies for you." She beamed.

"Get out, get out," I howled as I pushed her rudely out.

Three minutes later, Gamal knocked on the door and said that the "Americani" was in the garden and wanted to see me. I hadn't expected Bill would have the nerve to show up here so soon. All I could say was that either the man was unusually thick-skinned or that he hadn't grasped the situation.

I ran downstairs. Bill was sitting nonchalantly on the swing, cleaning his pistol.

"What are you doing here," I asked.

"Cleaning my pistol. Nice, isn't it? Bought it in Italy in exchange for some cigarettes." He held it up and stroked it. I didn't like this at all. In the villages rejected suitors killed all the time, and, what's more, they usually killed the girl.

Suddenly Bill fired straight up into the air. The pigeons raced madly round and round the house, the animals went berserk, the servants all rushed out of the kitchen, and the family appeared all over the balconies.

Bill just sat on the swing and roared with laughter.

"Mad, mad!" cried Mother.

"Mad, mad!" cried Father.

"*Magnoon, magnoon!*" chorused the servants. "Magnoon" is a beautiful Arabic word much used. It means "mad."

"Please go," I begged. "You make me nervous."

That afternoon, the relatives and friends paid us a visit. It seems they all happened to be passing by and thought they'd drop in and see Mother, but actually, it was more like the storming of the Bastille. I did not dare go downstairs and face the multitude, but just sat in my room surrounded by my good friends, waiting for the siege to end.

It was like that for a few weeks. People came to the house every afternoon, and Gamal was kept on his toes passing round the cups of Turkish coffee. The phone, of course, never stopped ringing. Everyone had some advice, some condolence to offer, as though we were bereaved. As for tragic stories of luckless girls who had been foolish enough to marry soldiers, why, they went back as far as the Crusades.

The one who was the least put out was Bill. I think he found it quite an experience. I could just see him telling

185

folks back home about what happened "when I tried to date a Lebanese girl." Anyway, he came round most days and we'd sit in the garden surrounded by a regular harem of English Girls' College girls.

And then—I don't know how it happened, except that when things are so bad, they just have to get better—the angry stalemate was over. After the first furious shock had worn off, Mother, Father, and Bill began to take to one another, as though they belonged to the same family. They liked one another. They discovered they had much in common. Bill was bright and quick-witted and Father, who was a brilliant man himself, appreciated this. He also, I believe, secretly admired the fact that Bill was going to earn his own living the hard way, unaided by family or money, as was usually the case in the East.

"The boy has guts," conceded Father. The only thing Mother and he now hoped was that I would adjust to the new life and be happy.

Having accepted the idea that I was going to marry an American, the numerous friends and relatives who were always in the background of our lives, like the chorus in a Greek play, couldn't have been nicer to us. Back they all trouped to the house to be served more coffee and tell more stories. But these were happy stories, about what wonderful husbands Americans were and how they put their women on a pedestal in the States.

Though Bill and I often mimicked and made fun of the Chorus, we were actually very fond of them. Basically, they were kind, generous, and affectionate, and though I suspect they must have been a little bored with life, they certainly meant no harm and had no malice.

186

12

"Maktoub"—It Was Written

WHEN BILL AND I LEFT FOR THE STATES, I NEVER DREAMED that six years later, almost to the day, Bill's job would bring us back to Egypt to live for a number of years in Cairo.

Zeinap, that product of modern Turkey but nevertheless still a fatalist, said it was *Maktoub* ("It was written"), for she firmly believed that no matter what you did, your fate had a way of catching up with you. Maybe so, or perhaps it was just that we had, as the saying goes, drunk of the waters of the Nile and so returned.

At all events, in November, 1952, Bill and I and Linda, our cute, fair-haired, brown-eyed daughter, boarded the TWA Constellation at New York on our way to Cairo. The stewardess, in a skirt too tight for her, but no doubt just right for the male population on board, proceeded to prance up and down dishing out glamour as though it was her mission in life. It would have been the usual kind of plane trip except for my thoughts, which were racing madly round and round my brain.

In a matter of hours, I would be revisiting Egypt again, seeing Mother, Father, Yvonne and Helen, and all my friends, though many of the Nice Eligible Girls had married into the British Army after all, and would not be there. It would be fun to go to one of those fabulous Alexandria cocktail parties again, dip into the tahina, and not have to sit on my hands to stop my talking with them.

So much had happened since I had left Egypt.

There had been the Palestine War, with its humiliating defeats and defective-weapons scandals brought about by corruption and inefficiency in high government circles.

There had been the dramatic abrogation of the 1936 Anglo-Egyptian Treaty and the outbreak of serious rioting.

And on July 26, 1952, there had been the burning of Cairo, which had petrified not only foreigners living in Egypt but Egyptians as well, and had done much to discredit Egypt in the eyes of the world.

Some months later, General Naguib and a group of Free officers had marched on Cairo and taken over the city without resistance or bloodshed. King Farouk had gone.

The "No Smoking" sign flashed on. We fastened our seat belts, and a few minutes later we touched down at Cairo International Airport.

As we came down the steps out of the plane and into the warm bright sun, the same little man from the travel agency who had sent us off some six years ago grabbed hold of our hand-luggage and explained apologetically that though he would be with us, we would have to do the passport formalities ourselves this time.

The customs shed was much the same as it had always been—shabby and unworthy of an important center like Cairo—but the officers who were examining the passports were neat, courteous, and efficient. On the wall was a large portrait of Mohamed Naguib.

"Are you here on a visit?" asked the officer. When Bill replied that he was going to work in Cairo, he smiled, stamped the passport, and gave it back to him.

"Don't forget to register with the police within three days," he said as he handed us three forms each.

I looked around for Mother and Father. They were standing just outside the customs precinct, smiling and trying to attract Linda's attention.

"You have to get a special pass to come in here," said the little man from the travel agency, "and your father didn't think it was worth it." Then he added, "Don't worry, don't worry, I'll get you through all right," as though we were about to smuggle a vast quantity of hashish into the country. "They know me here and they're good people."

I tried to tell him that we had nothing worth mentioning except Linda, but he kept repeating, "Don't worry, don't worry," until, by the time we reached the customs officials, he really had me quite worried.

"Have you anything to declare?" asked the customs official. "Gold, jewelry?"

Bill held the keys in his hands, ready to open the luggage, and I was just beginning to say that I had nothing to declare when the little man from the travel agency began to laugh and interrupted with, "Oh, my goodness, what could they possibly be bringing with them from Europe." Actually we had come from the United States. "Don't you know they ride bicycles instead of cars in Europe? Bread was even rationed there."

"My goodness," said the customs official again. "Allah be praised, we are really blessed in Egypt. We lack for nothing.

189

Is it true," he asked Bill, "that ice she fall from the skies in Europe?"

Bill replied that he was darned right it did, and he could have answered that in a certain London apartment we had had, the temperature she was below freezing, just like outside. Father, who was getting impatient standing waiting by the gate, demanded in a loud voice if anything was wrong.

"Don't worry, don't worry," cried out the little man from the travel agency to Father.

The customs official marked our suitcases with chalk, and shook our hands. He beckoned to a porter. About six of them appeared, but I didn't mind. How many times I had longed for a porter in Europe and the States when there hadn't been one in sight.

Now at last we were reunited with Mother and Father and Helen, all of us laughing and talking at once. It was only 9 A.M., but they had already driven up from Alexandria that very morning, even managing to arrive a whole hour before the plane was due, for Father had refused to spend the night in Cairo and be robbed of the fun of waking everyone up at 4 A.M.

As we walked towards the car, a man with a fez and gold teeth came running up, laughing—they laugh a lot in Egypt—and asked if we had had a good trip. His face was familiar.

"Remember Mahmoud?" asked Helen.

Of course, now it came back to me. He ran into people and they always turned out to be brothers of his.

"We've exhausted the supply of chauffeurs Alex has to offer," Mother said, "and now we're getting the same ones all over again."

We drove off. It was a beautiful day. I noticed these things now, though I never used to think of the weather when I lived in Egypt—but then I never used to think at all. We drove through Heliopolis—pale yellow and depressing; I never had liked it—and some twenty minutes later, having crossed the large square of Cairo Station, bustling with people as usual, we came to what had been Shepheard's Hotel.

"My God," said Bill. There was nothing. It had been completely razed to the ground.

"A friend of ours was staying here when they burned it," said Mother, "and no one has ever seen her again. You should hear some of the stories they tell. Karim was up in Cairo on business that day and from the Semiramis Roof he could see the BOAC offices burning down."

"If you had been here a few months ago," said Father, "you would have been able to see the empty lots where buildings had been. But new constructions have gone up very quickly."

I noticed that the names above the stores were written in Arabic as well as French, and many of them were only in Arabic. Others had stuck brown paper over Latin characters.

We had coffee in the little garden at Groppi's. There were few people about, for it was not yet ten, and no one really turned up before eleven. During the war, of course, it had been difficult to find a table at any time. Now, two Greek ladies, a man reading *Al Ahram,* and a group of Saudi Arabians in flowing robes and with eyes working overtime were the only ones around, but there were plenty of suffragis.

We drove to Alex along the Desert Road. Hardly anyone ever took the other road through the villages with the kids, chickens, carts, and water buffalos all over the place unless they really had to. I was enjoying the drive and the sight of

191

all that sand stretching as far as the eye could see, almost completely flat, with the empty barrels of tar on either side of the road. The sky was very blue and the sun shone radiantly, brazenly ignoring the fact that it was November. Then, in the distance, like a pool of water shimmering across the road—a mirage. One often saw them.

We had a quick coffee at the Rest House and set off again. The coffee was good but the ladies' room was as foul as ever and thick with flies.

The air grew cooler as we approached Alex, and suddenly Mahmoud was pressing furiously on the brakes, as a herd of camels with their young furry ones leisurely crossed the road. Linda squealed excitedly. She had never seen a camel before. Camels and Cadillacs. Always camels and Cadillacs, not only here in the middle of the desert, but right in the heart of smart Zamalek as well. I had never noticed them side by side before, until Mrs. James had one day pointed out the incongruous picture they made.

At Mariout, little Arab children stood on either side of the road holding out enormous bunches of bright red poppies and yellow daisies.

"They never last long once they have been picked," said Mother, anticipating what I was about to say. "Have you forgotten? They just shed their petals all over the place."

But we slowed down and all the children came running up, thrusting their bouquets into the car, jabbering away excitedly. One little girl was very pretty in a shapeless orange dress with a medal hanging from a chain round her neck. A black kerchief was round her head and wisps of curly hair bleached by the sun escaped from under it.

We bought all the flowers so as not to disappoint them, and,

192

as Mother had warned, there were petals all over the place, even on Mahmoud's fez, but the car was filled with color.

Some forty minutes later, we were entering Alexandria. Had the streets really always been that narrow? Was this the town which had seemed like the hub of the universe to me, whose gossip had so worried the Nice Eligible Girls; was this home now? "Home is where you are, not where your family is," Zeinap had once said.

"How does it feel?" asked Helen.

"Strange." Very strange to be back in the old familiar surroundings, to all outward appearances much the same, except for new buildings which had shot up here and there, and some stores which had had their faces lifted. Although here, too, the names of the stores were up in Arabic letters beside the Latin characters, the town was still a good deal more European-looking than Cairo. It had always been so, and the people in the streets were the usual melting pot of Europeans and Levantines, though I had heard that in recent months many had left for good.

On the terrace of the Mohamed Aly Club, the same group of acid-stomached gentlemen sat contemplating the well-dressed ladies coming out of the hairdresser's opposite, and the policeman stood in exactly the same spot placidly waving in the traffic on.

"Is Mimi still around?" I asked Mother. "Remember, she used to wear a different outfit every day and parade up and down Rue Chérif? To me, she is Alexandria personified."

"Yes, she most certainly is still around," Mother replied, "and what's more she still parks her car regularly on the wrong side of the street. Remember that? Right under the very nose of the policeman."

193

"Doesn't he give her a ticket?" asked Bill. I could just see Mimi if she tried that on Fifth Avenue. She probably would, too.

"No, he doesn't give her a ticket. Instead, he tells her that he will personally look after her car himself. She refers to him as 'my policeman.' "

"I thought things had changed out here," said Bill.

"They have," said Father, "but not that much."

It suddenly struck me that while I had been away for six years, riding subways, learning to adapt, getting a new outlook and sense of values, in Alexandria they had continued to live in a comfortable world of their own. The more things changed, it seemed, the more they stayed the same.

"Is Ahmed the beggar still around?" I asked.

"Very much so," said Helen.

"And Mademoiselle Stefanakis?"

"She came home only yesterday and is making me a really lovely dress. She had all her teeth pulled out because she didn't like them any more and just wanted to get a set of false ones, and now she's sorry." Helen laughed.

"And the old tennis pro at the Sporting Club?" He had given Father lessons when he was a boy.

"He's still around," Helen said. "What did you expect, anyway? A purge?"

"I guess I've been reading too many of those sensational evening newspapers," I said.

Clear of the Rue Fouad now, we were driving down the Abukir Road, clean and wide with its flowers and palm trees on either side. The English Girls' College and its green roof-tops, and the old Twelfth General Hospital, now an Egyptian university, were just visible enough to bring on a rush of memories.

194

At Sidi-Gaber, a woman in a pink bathrobe with curlers in her hair leaned over a balcony and lowered a basket on a string. She was buying tomatoes from a man with a donkey cart. We heard her scream in Arabic, "Don't give me any rotten ones like last time, you thief, you." I could just see her living in England during the rationing.

Barefoot, clad in that all-weather outfit, the galabia, a tiny little boy came out of the ironer's place holding a dress on a hanger, on his way to deliver it to its owner. Ironers worked hard in their little shops, often converted garages, ironing clothes all day and often half the night, spraying them with water they had drawn into their mouths. There were many of them around, even in the very poor districts. Their work was good, and they were quick and very cheap. They were among those things which made life in Egypt so comfortable and easy. For the price one paid to have a shirt laundered in Switzerland, one could buy a new one in Egypt.

Everywhere there were fine new buildings and apartment houses, even in Ramleh, that most residential of districts where before there had only been large villas and gardens. At this rate, it would not be long before the face of Ramleh was completely changed. And then, jammed in between a modern block and a regal mansion, as crude and as shabby as ever, was that Egyptian institution, the café. They sat as I remembered them, the cooks, the chauffeurs, and the suffragis in their white galabias, sipping little cups of coffee, playing backgammon, or just staring into space with their large black eyes amidst the wail of Arabic music. Some things never changed.

We turned left, up the hill with the flame trees, which were not flowering now, and there they were, standing at the garden gate on the lookout for the car, just as they used to when we were children and came back from the summer holidays. Gamal, his face very black, ageless; and Ahmed, the half-wit kitchen boy who had so many daughters he didn't know what to do; and Hanna the cook, whose horse never came in, with his chef's hat on the back of his head; and Mohamed, the philosopher who said flowers were human and never bloomed in the gardens of the wicked. And fatter, more monumental than ever, stood Maha, in an almond-green dress with yellow flowers on it and a string of gold bracelets on her plump wrists.

We got out of the car and they were greeting us, all smiles, using flowery words of welcome, which somehow I knew they meant, as we shook hands, and Maha was kissing me noisily, weeping as she always did, making me want to cry, too—though when I was a child, seeing her cry used to make me laugh. Yvonne, radiant as ever, appeared with her twin boys and Karim, heavier than I remembered him, but very much the successful young executive. They lived next door in the villa Karim's father had built them in his garden, and they had seen us from the window.

We went into the house that I remembered so well, laughing and talking loudly, and I had no sooner had time to take in the life-size portrait of Grandmother now hanging beside the other one of Grandfather, and the vase of arum lilies on the corner table, just where it used to be, when the sound of cars driving up made us rush to the windows. There they were, tumbling out of their vehicles, cascading into the house, that very same body of relatives and friends who used to come and see us off every summer and come and meet us again in the autumn, that battalion of aunts and uncles and cousins and cousins' cousins whom we made fun of, but whom we loved dearly all the same, and who attended all the weddings and funerals and cocktail parties in Alexandria.

"Chérie," they cried, as they came towards me in waves, with arms outstretched, "Chérie, how are you? We saw you coming down Rue Fouad, but you didn't see us. Look who we've brought along."

I had already seen. It was half of Alexandria.

"But how thin you are," they cried, passing me round to be kissed.

"But how fat you are," I thought.

There was much voluble excitement and the kissing continued for a while, for they were just as affectionate and just as overpowering as they had always been. They hadn't changed a bit. Aunt Georgette was still insisting, as she used to years ago, that I come and taste her incomparable figs, dried on her own terrace because the sun was better there than anywhere else in Alexandria.

We sat in the blue room, the blue room for the homecomings, and the little blue and gold cups of Turkish coffee were passed round by Gamal. The voice of Cousin Marie, the Pekinese, still went right through one like a dagger. Robert the Eligible, who had married a most Eligible girl after all, was telling us about the long staple variety of cotton, and Adèle's mother was saying how right they had been to insist on a dress-designing career for Adèle—she was doing very well in Paris—and who knows, they might all have to work soon, for times were changing, though to me, sitting here with all the relatives, it seemed as though they hadn't changed a bit. I felt as if I had never been away.

Gamal came round again, this time with a tray of mulberry syrup and dates covered in fine sugar. Mrs. James used to love dates; indeed, she had loved everything about Egypt. She had gone back to England after the war to join the Land Army and put Britain back on its feet. She had come down and spent a weekend with Bill and myself in London once and had talked the hind legs off a donkey about the crops and the potatoes and turnips she had picked, not so good as they should be, but that was because of that wretched Labor Government. It hadn't been necessary to ask for her stories from the West Indies, the repertoire had been on the tip of her tongue, as fresh and entertaining as ever, and the blouse we had admired had been made, as though we didn't know it, from the usual bits and pieces, and had we heard that her daughter's feet were now so big that she had to wear men's shoes. The house would not be the same since the death of Mrs. James.

All the other governesses had gone, too. They had been happy in Egypt, but it was high time, they felt, for that little cottage in the country with the souvenirs from Egypt on the mantelpiece, and the many memories of a lifetime in the East stored away in their hearts. They had never been replaced. It was the end of a chapter.

The talking went on and on, all of them conversing at once, loudly, gesticulating with their hands this way and that, and I was being asked what it was like to keep house in America. Was it true that there were no servants at all, Cousin Marie wanted to know, as she bit into a nice plump date. Not even someone to do the cooking, or a kitchen boy whom one could train? Couldn't I perhaps have found some nice woman, if the worse came to the worse, like her stupid Roberta, who always put her nylons back in the wrong drawer.

I shook my head. "But who used to make the beds?" she asked, alarmed, half of a date held delicately between two fingers, and when I told her that it was I, she clapped her hands to her cheeks and cried, "How difficult life is in other countries. But it will be the same here, too. That's what they call progress."

I did not enlighten her further as to who used to empty the garbage. Indeed, I had often wondered as I fried Bill's eggs and bacon in the morning what Hanna and Maha and Gamal would say if they could see me—they who had been so highly amused whenever I had been tempted to come down into the kitchen and bake a cake like the one in the beautiful advertisement I had just seen in the American magazine. As though real ladies ever came down to the kitchen, unless, of course, it was to scream at the servants. They had never allowed me to do more than translate the recipe into Arabic while they fell over one another getting ingredients, which half the time had nothing to do with the recipe anyway. Hanna would ask if I didn't approve of his cooking, Ahmed would throw in a handful of the wrong thing, and if I so much as tried to get off my chair, Maha would push me back and say that I would only soil my hands. "Darling," she'd cry, "what do you think you've got *us* for?"

Several coffees later, the relatives, having embraced us again, departed the same way they had come, en masse. That was what made them so overwhelming, for individually, they were dull and insignificant, with not much to say for themselves. At last I was able to unpack and wash the lipstick smears off my face and sit quietly with Mother and Father and Bill in the sunny room upstairs, watching the turtle-doves assiduously chasing one another on the lawn where Bill and I and Mrs. James had once sat drinking beer with the convalescents. Flies buzzed contentedly on the windowpane, rolling over in the late afternoon sun. That sunshine—was there ever anything like it?

Tomorrow the lunches, dinner parties, and cocktail parties in our honor would begin in earnest, but I had been told apologetically that they would be on a much smaller scale than I remembered them.

"Things have changed," they said. And next week Bill and I would go up to Cairo to look for an apartment.

I hoped that there would be no more visitors today, for it would be pleasant just to sit and relax, doing nothing in particular. Linda had disappeared with Maha, who was no doubt telling her crazy Lebanese legends, and Helen had gone out with friends.

"Have a good time, Dear," Mother said serenely. "One is only young once." How different things had been for me. There was nothing like time. It cured and it killed.

It was very quiet after the roar of New York traffic, and I slept well in my old room with the pictures of the School Hockey Eleven on the wall. The tomorrow I had looked forward to was today. Sunshine was pouring into my room and a thousand birds seemed to have rendezvoused to chatter excitedly in the eucalyptus tree.

Suddenly, a volley of hammering broke the stillness of the early Sunday morning. All was well. It was Father doing his home repairs. Presently, he would test the radio, taking out all its insides like an eager surgeon, and then he would start fixing the bells.

And then I heard the footsteps of Mohamed crunching along the gravel path beneath the window and into the wooden hut at the bottom of the garden.

I was home.

13

The Muddled East Merry-Go-Round

LINDA COULDN'T HAVE CARED LESS WHEN WE TOOK OFF THE following week to look for an apartment in Cairo. She had Mother for a slave; Father, a grownup who liked to take things to pieces, to play with; and Maha, who was more comfortable to sit on than a Dunlopillo cushion.

We took the green-and-white Misrair plane from tiny Nouzha Airport, and by 10 A.M. we were at the Opera Square. There was a lot of movement in the streets already. "This is really a city," said Bill. Aunt Lolotte's car and driver were waiting for us at the Misrair Terminal and, after having dropped Bill off at the office on Sharia Kasr-el-Nil, I went round to her house in Zamalek.

I rang the bell and her old Mahmoud opened the door. As soon as he saw it was I, he beamed, asked how I was, how Bill was, and how many children I had. When I said I had a girl, he said, *"Mash'Allah, Mash'Allah,* may Allah give you a son," and showed me into the salon.

In the corner of the large, handsome room filled with the valuable ornaments which I wouldn't care to have in my own house but which looked good in other people's, Aunt Lolotte sat busily sewing baby clothes. The table in front of her was filled with bootees, bonnets, jackets, and smocked dresses.

"They're for the orphanage," she said as she kissed me. "How is Bill?"

"Fine."

"Did you hear yourself say that?" she asked. "Your lovely English accent! Gone. What a crime." I laughed.

"So you are going to live in Cairo," she said. "Just imagine. She starts off in Alexandria and then comes to live in Cairo via New York. You'll love Cairo, though it's not what it was before. Remember those fabulous days? Unbelievable. If we told people about them, they'd think we were showing off. I couldn't ever live anywhere else."

Mahmoud came in with coffee and we continued to chat. "Things have changed, you know, Jackie," said Aunt Lolotte.

"That's what everyone seems to say."

"Some people, the ones with much to lose, moan and groan about this and that, and chiefly that they have lost their land, but have they stopped to consider that there has been a revolution and that whereas in the French and Russian revolutions, people not only lost everything but were massacred and guillotined, here, in a country where mobs ran riot, the revolution was accomplished without any bloodshed whatsoever? That's quite something."

"Very true," I said, "but you obviously don't own land, or you wouldn't talk like that."

"I don't, but I expect I shall be hit another way. However, I'm going to tell you something, Jackie. People with large incomes say that their days are numbered—four years, five, six maybe—and I'm inclined to agree with them, but I also say that although some people are going to suffer, and I'm one of them, the country is going to become a force to be reckoned with and it is going to come out on top. I'm no politician, but that's what I think. Anyway, let's go and find you an apartment. I take it you prefer to live in Zamalek because you'd like to be near the Club for Linda."

"Yes, I think so," I said.

"Shall we go, then?"

We circled Sharia el Gezira, which hugs the Club, and drove right down to the end of the island. In between the villas and all around the embassies standing in their carefully-tended gardens with the policeman outside his sentry box, sleek luxury blocks had sprung up like mushrooms all over Zamalek.

"Even a well-known British architect, who came out to Cairo on a job recently, told me that he was very favorably impressed with the buildings here. They build quickly and well," Aunt Lolotte said.

The apartment houses looked clean and well-kept. In the new blocks, the rent for an unfurnished apartment was higher than in the older buildings, where rent was cheap and key money required. But by Stateside and European standards, none of the apartments, furnished or unfurnished, were really expensive, though they were easily twice the price of those in Alexandria.

I asked Aunt Lolotte why it should be so, and she said it was because of all the Americans who paid so much more than anybody else and spoiled the market "as they do everywhere else, Chérie, though it is no doubt very tactless of me to say so in front of you." She added, "You tell Bill from me to bargain."

About two weeks later, when Bill and I had looked over some fifty apartments, furnished and unfurnished, we hit on a real beauty. It was a furnished six-room, two-bathroom apartment on Sharia el Gezira. The living room windows overlooked the Nile on one side and Gezira Sporting Club on the other, and there was a large balcony all round. According to Bill, there was only one thing missing, so he promptly went out to some pet shop he had already discovered in Zamalek and came back with a couple of men carrying an immense aquarium in which floated some stupid-looking little fish. They installed this the whole length of the living room wall. Linda, leaving a sobbing Maha behind, came up from Alexandria, and after that, life in Cairo began in earnest.

At an American Embassy party, we had met a charming young couple, Pat and Hank Logan, who told us their suffragi knew an excellent cook who was simply dying to work for Americans. When he came along, a pathetic little old Sudanese with watery eyes, he immediately said, "I didn't know Her Excellency the Madam was a Lebanese. I thought I was going to work for a real American family. But *Maalish*," he added, "there's nothing I can do if such is my destiny. Either you're lucky or you're not lucky in life. Isn't that so?" he inquired, looking very sad, and I said yes.

He asked for eight pounds a month and said he would eat in, for his wife and family were away in the Sudan and he hadn't seen them for five years, though he sent them money regularly. He would be a cook-suffragi, which meant that he would cook and wait at table and also clean the house. His name was Succar, or rather it was El Hag Aly Mohamed Salah Soliman, but everyone called him Succar. El Hag meant that he had made the pilgrimage to Mecca.

I had never kept house in Egypt before. At home in Alex, the servants had all been with us for some thirty years and were part of the family. Now, I was to find out what it was like to interview nannies and especially to be able to keep one.

I didn't find it necessary to advertise in the *Egyptian Gazette*. All I did was say quite casually to Pat Logan that I was looking for a nanny, and the next day, the word having sputniked round the group of nannies who sat at the Club, six women came to the door. One was Greek, the rest Egyptian, and they all said they could do everything. The first one we hired chiefly because she wasn't as fat as the others. She was called Lou-Lou, pronounced as though one has hiccoughs, and she couldn't do anything. She stayed a week. One day, I noticed that she was wearing one of my best dresses to go out on her weekly day off, and when I said to her, "Lou-Lou, isn't that my dress?" she said, "Yes, Madam, my waist is exactly the same as Your Excellency's."

The next one stayed about six weeks, during which time we were answering the phone half the night. "It's my brother Youssef," she always said. "He is a son of a dog and he doesn't want me to work." One day her brother Youssef, who turned out to be her husband, came to the door and right then and there gave her a hearty beating, which nearly killed her, and took her away sobbing.

The third one was called Bahia, and I have since discovered that her kind of story is by no means unique. She was fat and she had one good eye.

"Ask her if she's married and if her husband allows her to work," said Bill when she came to be interviewed.

So I did.

"Married?" she cried. "Me?" She raised her one good eye to heaven. "I hate men. I never go near men. I never have anything to do with them." And for the next hour she elaborated in no uncertain terms about the wretchedness of men.

"Ask her what's the matter with her stomach," Bill said. "It's kind of, well, a little big, don't you think?"

"You ask her," I said. "All these women's stomachs are a little big. I don't know why it is, but it's a fact. Big stomachs and big rear ends."

"Don't chicken out," said Bill. "Ask her or I'll say 'I divorce you' three times." He was picking up the least attractive of the local customs.

"No wonder she won't have anything to do with men, if they're all like you," I said. "All right, I'll ask her."

So I asked her, and she said it was wind.

"There you are. See?" I said. "You made me a look a fool. It's nothing. Just wind."

"O.K. Hire her," said the Sultan of Zamalek. "And get me a drink, will you, and go easy on the soda, because I've been drinking too much these days," he added with logic. The way I looked at it, it was pointless marrying an American if he was going to lord it like an Oriental.

Some three weeks later, Bahia, kohl smeared round the eyes as though she were about to go on the stage, and wearing a blinding bilious-green dress which she kept referring to as sky blue, left as usual for her Friday off.

"Please be sure not to get back too late tomorrow morning," I said, as she opened the door to leave. "I have several things to do."

"*La, la, la, la*—no, no, no, no," she assured me. "I'll be here first thing, before you are even awake."

First thing a week later she still had not returned or given any sign of life, which didn't really upset my plans much. I only missed two drawing lessons, two bridge lessons, three lunches, four dinners, five cocktail parties, and a miserable little desert party. However, three weeks later, the bell rang while we were having lunch, and in came Bahia, holding a baby on each arm. "Saida," she said. It means good morning, good afternoon, good day, and, like the galabia, it can be used anytime.

"Saida," we said.

"Ask her whose they are and where she's been," said Bill.

So I did, and she told me that they were hers, and she pointed out that one of them had blue eyes and so she had decided to call him Bill, but the one with black eyes she was calling Mohamed.

"But why didn't you tell me you were married?" I asked her.

"I'm not," she replied. "I never lie. Didn't I tell you I hated men?"

"What is she saying?" Bill wanted to know.

"She says she's not."

"She's not what?"

"Married, of course."

And then Bahia started to tell us some incoherent story about a Coca-Cola truck driver who, we gathered, had run over her, but what could she do, Your Excellency, when he was her own uncle? Apparently her uncle was getting a good salary and wanted to marry her, but she didn't like men. And she didn't like Coca-Cola.

"Well, when can I return?" she asked.

"How can we take you back," I asked her, "when for a start you have the twins?"

"What, those little things? Don't worry about them. I'm giving one away to a relative in Mansourah, and the other my daughter is going to look after."

"You've got a daughter?" I asked her, surprised.

"Of course I have a daughter," she said, and laughed. "Why shouldn't I have a daughter?"

"What did she say, what did she say?" asked Bill.

So I told him. For once Bill said nothing, but because he had given up drinking, he just went over to the bar and poured himself a very stiff Scotch.

Whatever one could say of keeping house in Cairo, I, for one, never found it dull. Nor did my everyday friends, Pat Logan, Jane Brown, another American Embassy wife, and Betty May, an English girl whose husband Peter was with the Eastern Tobacco Company. Peter was a good-looking young man, very English, and of course devoted to cricket, which he played every Sunday at the Club in impeccable white flannels and in a 110-degree temperature.

Jane Brown was one of those Americans who come from Alabama and sound like it. She always wore American dresses and American glasses, Italian shoes, and long Musky earrings, and then wanted to know how everybody guessed she was American. She was thrilled to bits to be in Egypt, "where it all began," and talked of the Ancient Egyptians as though they were all my nearest relatives. The key of life obsessed her, and she saw weird symbols even in the rolled vine leaves.

The four of us regularly met for morning coffee at one of our houses, and the conversation invariably got around to the nannies, suffragis, and boabs, or doormen. Often we'd forget the time in the midst of hilarious anecdotes, and Bill would come home to find us all prostrate with laughter over some of the incredible stories of life with Fatima and Mohamed.

Bill said I had a positive genius for attracting characters,

208

for we had yet another one in the household. She was Om Mahmoud, the washerwoman.

When she came, once a week, she'd take off her black shroud, revealing a shapeless bulk clad in an equally shapeless white sack-dress with frayed edges. She was always barefoot, summer and winter, and the soles of her feet were like leather. Then she'd ask after His Excellency the Pasha. This was Bill. Even though titles had been abolished, they were still used, especially when speaking to people who had never had one. It was a form of flattery and there was nothing sarcastic in it at all.

When I'd tell her that he was away in the villages on business, she'd say: "Is that so?" and give me a knowing look out of the corners of her very black eyes, after which she'd tell me that she happened to know he was spending nights under the spell of some green-eyed she-devil, who, she'd add, "is, like Your Excellency, a Lebanese. And, with all respect to Your Excellency," she'd say, "you know the Lebanese."

One day she came along as usual and, from the folds of her black *milaya,* produced a messy package wrapped in an Arabic newspaper. She said it was a magic powder she had obtained from the famous Om Aly of Giza, so famous no one had ever heard of her. It hadn't been easy to obtain this powder which no one had asked her for, and she had had to give Om Aly one whole pound.

"On my eyes," she swore shrilly, nearly poking them out with her two fingers, "I have great affection for Your Excellency," which was as good as saying she knew a fool when she saw one. I was to be sure and sprinkle all the powder into Bill's bath—without his seeing me do it, however—and repeat his name twelve times, because he was born on the twelfth of December. This would break the spell and make him stay home.

It wasn't difficult convincing easygoing Bill that he didn't really want a shower, especially since I had prepared him a nice warm bath like the good dutiful slave that I was, and I had thrown the powder, which looked like flour mingled with black watermelon seeds, into the bath water.

Instead of working like black magic, the powder worked like a powerful white detergent, and the bathroom was filled with soapsuds overflowing onto the floor, climbing up the walls, crawling over the mirror, and reaching the ceiling. Bill grabbed me by the arm, demanding to know, in the most dreadful language I had yet heard him use, what in the name of something quite unmentionable I had done with his bath water. Looking at all the foam, with the bits of black watermelon seeds rising by the second, I said that I couldn't see anything unusual in the sight of the bathroom at all.

But it was a delight, after all the housework in London and the States, to have Succar, no matter how stupid he was, to do the marketing, cooking, and cleaning. He was a wonderful man, willing, devoted, and very honest, but his mind worked something like this:

"Succar," I'd say, "this table is dusty."

Some few hours later, I'd discover that the table was still dusty, so I'd say, "Succar, didn't I tell you the table was dusty?"

"Yes, Madam," he'd reply, seriously, not cheekily, "but you didn't tell me to clean it."

Sometimes, exasperated at his stupidity, I'd cry, "But Succar, how can you be so stupid?" And he'd answer most pathetically, looking at me with his watery eyes, which he said had got that way from steamy kitchens, "But Madam, don't you know our brain is not like yours. Our brain is small—as small as a bird's," he'd explain gently. "We don't think like you. Our minds are very simple. We just eat, sleep, work, pray, that's all."

Succar did not approve of my housekeeping, and once, when he had sulked for several days and cooked us the opposite of everything we had asked for, I inquired if there was anything wrong. After a lot of hemming and hawing, he finally said, shaking his head sadly, "You are not a real lady; you don't come into the kitchen and shout at me regularly like all the other ladies do." So, after that, once a week, I made a point of finding something to have a real row about, even threatening to fire him, so that Succar could boast to his friends in the café that he worked for the most terrible lady in all Zamalek.

It was fun to do the pleasant things around the house, like arranging the flowers, or picking up the phone to order food from Groppi's and Lappa's.

"Succar," I'd say, "we're having three people for dinner tonight," and Succar, his honest face a complete blank, would reply, "Yes, Madam," and then immediately go and lay the table for thirteen, and when I'd say, "Succar, we'll be thirteen for dinner tonight—thirteen, Succar, not three," Succar would reply, "Yes, Madam," and then go and lay the table for three. After each party, he picked up a glass and smashed it on the kitchen floor—to keep the devil away from the house, he explained.

Some of my European friends got their suffragi to bring them breakfast in bed every morning. "We're only here for a two-year tour," they'd say, "and now, with a nanny, we

211

don't have to get the children up for school. We'll never have this sort of thing again, so we may as well get the most out of it." People always wanted to get the most out of Egypt.

From the point of view of easy living and comfort, I couldn't see that Egypt had changed at all. It was as the customs official had said, a blessed country, where the weather was kind, and where one could still buy a large helping of brown beans and bread for something like two cents. Foods such as rice and vegetables were cheap. So were clothes, shoes, labor, and a good seat at the movies. Bill's Arabic teacher, who only earned eighteen pounds a month, had a young woman servant who slept on the floor and earned one and a half pounds a month.

Everywhere, one was waited on hand and foot. Zamalek abounded with ironers, grocers, cleaners, cobblers, gas stations, carpenters, upholsterers, florists, invisible menders, and bakeries. I rarely went downtown to do my shopping. Regularly, I went to the beauty parlor owned by a Greek in Zamalek. I never made an appointment because I had discovered long ago that time has no meaning in this part of the world. I just went along when it suited me. Mr. Taky would send for a coffee from Simmond's and glance about his tiny salon to see whether he could perhaps fit me in between two Iron-Curtain-Country wives. Then he'd give me his special: a summary of the week's political situation in a couple of deft snips.

The months flew by, and we enjoyed living in Cairo. Bill worked from eight till two and then had the rest of the afternoon in which to play golf or do anything he pleased. It was a far cry indeed from the nine-to-five routine he had had before. In winter it had been dark when he came out of the office, and there had been no time for any kind of sport. Over the weekend he had tried to get in a game of golf—weather permitting—but even then, the golf course was several miles away, and he couldn't afford a caddy. Now, it was a treat to laze in the sun at Gezira Sporting Club, dip into the pool, and then just call any of a multitude of suffragis to bring lunch or a bottle of beer, or just run and fetch you a pack of cigarettes.

Now at last, there was time for those piano lessons, for the bridge and the sketching classes, for coffee parties, moonlight parties, felucca parties on the Nile, and just time to enjoy living. Before, I had taken all these things for granted. Now, after having lived abroad, I appreciated them.

Bill and I liked to have a few friends in for a drink and sit on the balcony overlooking Gezira on one side and the Nile on the other, clinking the ice cubes in the highball glasses. After the dry heat of day, the balmy evening air felt good on one's sun-tanned skin, and while we talked of subjects ranging from the menace of International Communism to the price of chicken wings at Ataba Market, the thin crescent of the new moon hung delicately in the sky, and the plaintive notes of a flute wafted over from one of the feluccas. We were all very happy in Cairo.

Pat and Hank Logan specialized in desert parties, which they usually threw as a farewell to any of their friends who were leaving Egypt. Inside the tent with the kaleidoscope colors and Persian rugs which they had some miles beyond the Pyramids, an immense table groaned with grilled lamb chops, chicken livers, kebab, kofta, and tahina.

Outside on the sand, chairs and leather hassocks were arranged in a large circle, and the Bedouins would play their

213

slightly off-key, off-beat music on their weird instruments and drums fashioned of earthenware pots covered with goat's hide. The rhythm would change to yet another uncanny accent, and presently the dancing horses would come on, adorned with pompons and ridden by dark-skinned Bedouins in turbans and white robes. Proudly, the Arab horses pranced round and round while the music, following its sinuous course, enveloped one completely.

Later in the evening, off everyone would go on camelback, racing each other—camels can run very fast—across the miles of soft sand, and sometimes when I looked up there would be a shooting star blazing across the indigo sky. In the light of the moon, the three Pyramids would appear ghostlike before us, and even at this distance, several miles from the tent, the beat of the drum would come drifting over.

Sometimes we stayed to watch the sunrise, and then we'd get into the cars and drive back to Zamalek.

Unlike that in many Moslem countries, night life in Egypt was good, and there was a choice of several first-class restaurants and night clubs to go to, not cheap, but not expensive. We particularly liked the roof of the Semiramis Hotel with its view of the shimmering Nile—I like the sight of water at night—and anchored nearby, the Omar Khayyam, where one sat in Oriental surroundings and ate kebab as one watched the moving lights on Kasr-el-Nil Bridge. There was the verandah of the Mena House Hotel, with its excellent Italian band and lights camouflaged up in the palm trees, and, down the road, the Auberge des Pyramides, where one could take in a good floor show and see a really expert belly dance.

As soon as the acrobats or the inevitable chanteuse—that typical night-club act the world over—had taken a last bow amidst a cacophony of discordant sounds, a group of nonde-script looking men came on carrying their own chairs, as though they were too unimportant for anyone to bother with. Unhurried, they'd sit down, adjust themselves a little, and then the man with the drum would start that off-beat going with his fingers. It had begun. As the other instruments joined in, an "ah" of expectancy would go round the audience, and suddenly the dancer would appear, snakelike, clothed in a scant vaporous outfit inlaid with gold and silver threads and beads round the neck, and for the next fifteen minutes she would captivate all the tired businessmen, tourists, and diplomats of Cairo with that most suggestive of all dances.

The next day, Pat, Betty and I would be inquiring where we could take belly-dancing lessons.

Soon, it was the month of Ramadan again—a little earlier each year, for the Mohammedan year is a lunar one. Rama-dan, the month of abstinence and prayer, is very widely ob-served in Egypt, and I have often seen the very devout take off their shoes and pray in the crowded Diesel that journeys between Alexandria and Cairo. During the day, work slows down—the cynics say it is at a standstill—the little cups of Turkish coffee are not passed round the offices, for no one drinks or eats from sunrise to sunset, and Succar's brain ceases to function altogether. But no one ever complains about the holy month of Ramadan.

Just before sunset, the streets are suddenly deserted, and the bustling, noisy city looks almost dead. Even the police-man has disappeared for a few minutes to buy his plateful of brown beans.

Bill's Arabic teacher said one day, "I pray the Jews never attack us at this hour just before the Iftar."

From the minaret comes the clear voice of the muezzin chanting the praises of Allah, and those who are still around the streets cluster in little groups waiting to hear the sound of the cannon which will announce the breaking of the fast. As soon as it is heard, there is much excitement. Children who had been sent to watch the minaret or listen for the guns come racing back, and they all sit cross-legged on the pavement outside their dark little stores, the *makwagi* and the tailor, the ex-pasha's driver, and the Bedouin woman who sells eggs on the street corner, and the dark-haired, barefooted kids, all dipping their bread into the platefuls of beans and crunching the spring onions.

During Ramadan, the city lives by night, for that is the time when one can eat and drink. Colored lamps are hung everywhere, but especially in the poorer quarters, and the cafés are packed with people drinking amareddine, a very sweet apricot syrup which as a rule is drunk only during Ramadan. And, of course, the music from the loud-speakers blares out more stridently than ever. Since they have another meal just before the sun rises, people often sit up and revel all night and don't get to bed until dawn.

Bill and Hank Logan were invited to an Iftar by some Egyptian friends, and they had been told that they would appreciate the Iftar much more if they ate very little during the day. Bill and Hank decided they would do things properly and observe the complete fast from sunrise to sunset. By the end of the morning, Bill's throat was parched and he was in a wretched mood. He hadn't had his coffee, and he hadn't had his Camels, and he'd fired all the clerks. When he came home at two and found me sitting having lunch with Linda, he said, "Whenever I see you, you're eating," and after some more unsolicited remarks he finally went to bed and slept until five-thirty. Hank Logan, who according to Pat had acted exactly the same way, called for him at a quarter to six, and the two of them set off hungrily for their Iftar. Pat and I, who were to spend the evening together, were very glad to see them go.

Their meal lasted some two hours, and there was everything one could possibly imagine in the way of food—turkeys, pigeons, fish, chicken—but there were no alcoholic beverages, for they are forbidden by the Moslem religion. Instead, there was amareddine and Coca-Cola. At the end of the meal, some of the forty people present got up and prayed in a corner of the room, unselfconscious, and the others continued to talk or just sat and watched. Later on in the evening, Bill and Hank were taken to Fishawi's in the Musky, where, amid a multitude of colored lamps hanging from the ceiling, they sat and drank green tea. They didn't get home until nearly dawn.

In his work, Bill met many Egyptians, average, decent, middle-class people who were always friendly and ready to help. Egyptians are very hospitable, and the poorer they were, the more hospitable and the more they plied him with food whenever he went to have lunch with them. I didn't go along, for the womenfolk were never present. The Egyptians were pleased that a foreigner like Bill genuinely liked their country, and there wasn't enough they could do for him.

One day, Bill and Peter May came home from a Bedouin wedding to tell us that their host, the bride's father, had ordered a tree to be chopped down with one command of the hand, because he thought it interfered with Bill's view of

217

the dancing. "You are a guest," sad the bride's father, "and must be honored like one."

Though life in Egypt was easy compared to that in some other parts of the world, I noticed the new spirt of pride with which Egyptians spoke of their country since the revolution. The bulk of the people—the clerks, lawyers, students, cab drivers—the average middle-class Egyptian, who had been ashamed of the reputation his country had acquired abroad, approved of the new regime's fight against corruption and the measures taken towards social reform. Hardly anyone regretted the departure of King Farouk. Sometimes the propaganda was a little crude, but it had to be simple to get across to the mass of the people. The politicians who had regarded power as a means of filling their own pockets and supplying members of their families with government jobs were out, and in their place were young men who, if without much experience, at least had a new sense of duty and were putting the country first. One felt as though swept by a strong current, a new driving force. Everywhere, in all the stores and offices, there were pictures of Mohamed Naguib, who, perhaps because of his fatherly face, had become very popular with the people. A helicopter landed in the middle of Gezira Sporting Club one day and distributed photographs of him. At the movies, audiences joined in wholeheartedly to sing the patriotic songs exhorting union, discipline, and work, and cheered spontaneously whenever the revolutionary leaders appeared on the screeen. Stores began to have such names as "Honesty" and "New Regime."

The Arabic language became more and more indispensable in business. Foreign technicians were welcome as long as they trained Egyptians to be able to replace them in the near future. In the French- and English-language newspapers, ads stressing that applicants should have Egyptian nationality were more frequent. It was those who had lived in Egypt all their lives and still spoke only kitchen Arabic who were to suffer most. But for the first time in the history of the long-suffering Egyptian people, being Egyptian was no longer a liability, and the Egyptian, who had always had to play up to the foreigner, was at home in his own country.

Yet, strangely enough, at first there was no feeling of vengeance, no fanaticism against Europeans in the streets for instance, no riots as in the olden days. It was as though the Egyptians wanted to show that they were perfectly capable of self-discipline too. It was commendable and touching, too, to see Boy Scouts all over the town showing people how to cross the streets in an orderly manner and how to obey the traffic lights.

Bill's Arabic teacher said to him, "The regime has inherited an awful mess. We have a great deal of work to do. Sure we'll make mistakes, but they'll be honest ones, and we'll learn. We want to put our own house in order by ourselves. When it's your own house, you work with a will."

It was the minority, and many of our friends were among them, who moaned and groaned that their income was going to be amputated, that after the land reform and the law on rents it would be something else, and who spoke of the good old days when they could travel to Europe with as much money as they liked. The mass of the people had never been abroad and were not likely to go. If certain items were beginning to be scarce in the stores because there was no foreign currency with which to purchase them from abroad, they were not the things that our nanny, Fathia, or Bill's Arabic

219

teacher would be likely to buy, and it was people like them, after all, who comprised the bulk of the population. Egypt is an agricultural country and there was always bread, rice, and vegetables, and now, in addition, there was price control. As for certain luxury articles which had gone up in price— American cars and whisky, for instance—the rich, though they naturally grumbled, could still afford to buy them.

It was not easy to foretell how things would go, whether the regime would be able to surmount all the obstacles, but certainly the spirit of a renaissance was there. Egyptians were closer to one another than they had ever been before, and there was new hope for a people who for years had been humiliated, belittled, and abused. I had the very definite impression that it was as though a giant was awakening and its potentials were immense.

By the end of 1954, Egypt, both politically and otherwise, was well in the center of the world stage. Colonel Abdul Nasser, who was said to have been the brains behind the 1957 revolt, had relieved General Naguib of his functions, not for the first time. An important relic of Ancient Egypt, a wooden solar bark belonging to the Pharaoh Cheops, had been discovered near the Great Pyramid at Giza, and even the Miss World Beauty Contest in London had been won by a girl from Cairo.

Naguib was accused of having plotted against the life of Gamal Abdul Nasser with the help of the outlawed Moslem Brotherhood, and he just faded out of the picture. But the government forged ahead with its immense task of developing local industries, increasing the national production, and trying to raise the standard of living. As for the city of Cairo itself, it underwent a beauty treatment.

"Fancy spending all that money for a fountain to spout water in the middle of the Nile," grumbled Om Mahmoud, the washerwoman. She criticized everything, and she didn't think, like Fathia the nanny, that man does not live by bread alone.

A new Corniche along the Nile was cut through from Choubrah to Maadi and Helouan in a matter of weeks, and new luxury hotels—Shepheard's and the Hilton—were being built overlooking the Nile. There were ambitious plans for irrigation schemes, new bridges, port facilities, and a city on the Mokattam Hills, with a gambling casino to attract tourists. (Only foreign nationals; no Egyptians were allowed to gamble.) The royal palaces were opened to the public, and the Abdine Palace night club was crowded most nights. Cairo was growing fast, while Alexandria appeared to get smaller every time we visited it, quite lost in a little world of its own.

Bill had an Egyptian friend, a young lawyer who was doing well now that so many new laws were being passed. He said to Bill, "Americans at least surely understand how we feel. They fought to get rid of the British, too."

Our new nanny, Fathia, a nice girl who represented the shape of things to come, was very interested in politics and the world around her. Every evening after she had put Linda to bed, she liked to listen to the radio, not just to the ESB from Cairo, but also to the Voice of America. The day the Egyptian flag was hoisted in the Canal Zone she said, "Isn't it wonderful that these people have accomplished in a few months what all the others hadn't been able to do in years?"

When the day came to elect a president of the Republic, Fathia was very excited and took the day off to go to the polls in her district of Sayeda Zeinab. She was very pleased when

Colonel Nasser was elected President by over 99 per cent of the votes, but she was also a little baffled. She had heard that in other countries there was more than one candidate, and she came to ask Bill if this was true.

But by July, 1956, I could tell when I paused to breathe between one cocktail party and another that the situation in the Middle East was what is politely known as "strained." One could judge how great a power was by the number of attachés who were being expelled.

The West, whose strong point was not the Middle East, accused Egypt of going Communist because Egypt, having been refused Western arms, had concluded a deal with the Soviet bloc. The Baghdad Pact was considered in Egypt an imperialist scheme to interfere in other countries' affairs, and was held in low repute. So was France, for its butchery in Algeria. So was Great Britain, for its policy in Cyprus and because it was always held responsible for everything. So was the U.S., which had refused Egypt arms, but had supplied the French NATO units with arms which were apparently being used to crush the Algerian rebels or patriots, according to whose side one was on. The members of the Arab family were at daggers drawn, all except Egypt and Syria, who were vaguely talking of marriage but were being accused by the West of being gluttons for the Russian Salad. Happy-go-lucky Lebanon was making whoopee out of it all; for how long, nobody knew, but it was in hard currency. Israel, the bête noire, was playing her favorite game of "Over the Border." Shepilov, who had come over to Egypt for the evacuation festivities, was whispering sweet nothings into his host's ear—all about a high dam, of all things—while poor Mr. Hammarskjöld flew around with his little olive branch. Meanwhile, President Nasser, who was proving himself more astute than the West had expected, continued to denounce imperialism and reaffirmed that he stood by the Bandung principle of positive neutrality and nonattachment to blocs. In July, the Big Three champions of peaceful co-existence—India, Yugoslavia, and Egypt—met in Belgrade, and the next day, when I looked at the papers, I read that some poor woman had given the names of Tito, Nasser, and Nehru to her newborn triplets. She got nice gifts.

There was a Russian exhibition on at Gezira in Cairo, and there had been a Red Chinese one as well, and the word "Communism" was beginning to go the rounds. In the red hammer-and-sickle flags flying beside those of Egypt the whole length of the Kasr-el-Nil Bridge, some, mostly the well to do, saw the sinister hand of the Kremlin taking a grip on the country. "You see, you see," they whispered, "we understood the writing on the wall long ago. Didn't we tell you four years ago, or maybe five? People like us are finished."

Bill's Egyptian friend, the young lawyer, said, "How can the West really believe that we are going over to Russia? Don't they realize that after all these years when we had to run to Lord Cromer if we so much as wanted a bag of peanuts, we are not about to jump from a British occupation into a Russian one? Nasser is not a Communist and there is no Communist party. We just want to be left to ourselves, like Switzerland. Is that so bad?"

"But look at all the influx of Russian things," Bill said.

"You mean all those Soviet magazines?" asked the lawyer. "I'm not worried. We just use them to wrap our bananas in." He laughed. "We prefer to pay a little more and read things like *Tit Bits* and *Confidential.*"

But for all that, as the Nile began to rise in late July of 1956, the atmosphere in Cairo became more sullen and full of foreboding. The kites prowling overhead looked more ominous than usual, and the radios took on a belligerent tone. The group of crinkly-haired nannies sitting at the club with their fair little charges, talked as shrilly as ever, but in some salons they were whispering. Even our parties had lost their sparkle and were falling somewhat flat.

Then, suddenly, the elastic snapped. The U.S. withdrew its offer to finance the Aswan High Dam. Britain played Follow the Leader, and the Arab giant of nationalism, now thoroughly aroused, was very angry.

14

Speak To Me of Suez

IT WAS THE FOURTH ANNIVERSARY OF THE REVOLUTION, AND together with friends, we had decided to spend the holiday by the Red Sea. Dave Berry of the American Express, one of our crazy Cairo friends, was organizing the expedition. Some of the others were from the American Embassy. It was a very congenial group we had in Cairo in 1956, the kind one only comes across once in a blue moon and remembers for the rest of one's life. On looking back, it does seem strange to have had so many screwballs in one place at the same time.

At blistering noon, we set off, Bill and I in the Logans' station wagon. There were four other cars and an old blue truck which belonged to Dave, into which we had thrown the tents, sleeping bags, iceboxes, water coolers, underwater equipment, and enough food to last a pack of hungry wolves for three days. The truck was a typical Dave Berry acquisition, a monstrosity with no doors—they had dropped out like old teeth—and no spare. Dave had another car, an old second-hand Studebaker which he never kept in a garage and which he flatly refused to have cleaned. Even Linda knew it when it went by and disdainfully looked the other way. Every so often, he'd somehow manage to run out of gas a block away from the Gezira Sporting Club, and there he'd stand, waving frantically, trying to attract the attention of any of his friends who might be passing by. Like my bridge, it was a severe strain on friendship.

We drove through the teeming streets of Cairo. People were everywhere—milling along the Nile Corniche in bright pajamas and gaudy pink satin dresses, sitting in the gaily festooned feluccas, squatting in the Ezbekieh Gardens with their flocks of children, and clustering like ants at the feet of the statues. Triumphal arches, all of them bearing slogans, had been put up in the main streets, and though they were fun, what they did to traffic wasn't.

Finally, we were on the Suez road. We stopped at a couple of check-posts to show our passes, and from then on drove mostly along the sea. Some four hours later, we cut across the sand and pitched our tents. It was a perfect spot Dave had brought us to, a testimony to his many weekends by the Red Sea. Barren limestone ranges stretched behind us, and though there were shingles by the water's edge, the sand was white and smooth.

We put on bathing suits, and, looking like characters from outer space in our snorkels, we ran into the water and made for the dark patches which indicated the presence of coral reefs. We wore old tennis shoes so as not to cut our feet on the coral. I looked down just below the surface of the water, and found myself in a fascinating world of fish. There were myriads of them swimming about, for the most part small, but of every shade one could possibly imagine. Some were jet-black, many had bizarre patterns, and for once, I could understand what Bill saw in fish.

We were up early the next morning, leaving those who swore they never slept a wink all night still snoring away, and we were in the water before breakfast. The day raced by, as time has an uncanny habit of doing when you don't want it to. We looked at the coral reef again and again, speared some fish, saw a squadron of dolphins, and drank ice-cold beer. This was the life. Nature, but not quite in the raw. You'd never catch an American drinking warm beer, even in the middle of the desert.

In the evening, we sat round a huge fire, feeling very happy, contented, and sunburnt. I saw a couple of shooting stars. Somebody switched on a portable radio, and an absolute flurry of angry words and tumultuous applause came tumbling about my ears.

"It's Nasser's speech," I said. I had quite forgotten about that.

"What's he saying?" queried voices.

"This Canal is an Egyptian Canal," cried President Nasser, and again there was tumultuous applause.

I could imagine President Nasser standing in Alexandria, my home town, in the middle of Liberation Square. I could visualize him telling the people the story of the Canal, their Canal. He liked to emphasize words and was very easy to understand, for he spoke colloquial Arabic, the kind one speaks to a friend. And I could just see the faces around him. Many would have come from the villages in trucks to cheer the President.

The voice was getting louder and more excited, the cheering more prolonged.

"What is he saying?" everybody wanted to know.

"He says they won't let imperialists dominate Egypt. They will build a dignified Arab Egypt," I said quickly, anxious not to miss a single word.

227

President Nasser then read the text of the decree national-izing the Suez Canal Company. As he spoke, the Canal was being taken over by Egyptians. "May Allah guide you and peace be with you."

We switched off the radio in the midst of thunderous ap-plause which made the radio reverberate. Tomorrow, more than the radio would reverberate.

We sat quietly for some seconds, the cheering still re-sounding in our ears, and only the waves continued un-changed. Then we all started to talk at once.

"He can't do that," said Peter May.

"Well, he just has," I reminded him.

Stunned, that's what we were.

"What did he say about America?" Dave wanted to know.

"He said may you choke to death on your fury," I told him.

"Thanks," said Dave.

"For Pete's sake, it's an international waterway," cried Peter. He was upset.

"It's also an Egyptian Company," somebody answered. Everyone put in a word.

"It's highway robbery," said one.

"He'll climb down," said Peter.

"Bet you he doesn't," said another.

We talked for hours, accomplishing and solving nothing, and then went to bed.

The next morning, we decided to cut our holiday short and return to Cairo right away. We had left Linda with Fathia, the young nanny, and one never knew what might happen now. Although there had been no riots under the new regime, I felt that President Nasser's speech might un-

228

leash nationalistic passions and all my old fears of mob vio-
lence returned.

During the drive back to Cairo, we twiddled the knob on
the radio, tuning in to every possible news bulletin, and in
all of them the Suez Canal—literally a few miles away from
where we were—held the most prominent place. The far-
reaching implications that the nationalization of the Suez
Canal would have were coming home to us.

When we got back to Cairo, the city still wore its festive
air, and there were many people about the streets, just wan-
dering around doing nothing in particular as though waiting
for something more to happen.

Good old Succar, like a faithful old dog, was asleep on the
chair in the kitchen. When we came in, he awoke with a
start, tottered over to the stove, and with his bare hands
scooped a couple of eggs out of the boiling water. He did it
so often, I had ceased to be amazed long ago. Linda was painting ships all over the walls of the corridor, and Fathia was
listening to Cairo Radio, which one could hear clear out in
the street. In short, all was normal.

"Have you heard the wonderful news about the Canal?"
Fathia asked excitedly. "To think that we've been robbed all
these years. But we are free of imperialists now. May Allah
grant Gamal long life."

I don't really know what I had expected her to say.

For the next few weeks, the tension in Cairo mounted
steadily while nations joined in a slugging match. Notes and
protests flew back and forth. The British, French, and U.S.
fleets then began to take precautionary measures in the Mediterranean, which reassured British, French, and American
subjects but only helped to convince Egyptians that they, a

small nation, were being bullied and intimidated by three powerful ones.

In August, a twenty-two power conference was called in London. It is inadmissible, cried Britain, France, and other Western nations, that any single country should have sole control of the Canal. It is inadmissible, cried President Nasser in return, that they should meet to discuss an integral part of Egypt, and he refused to attend.

Bill, Linda, and I still spent every afternoon swimming and sunbathing at the Club. It was a very warm summer, sticky and oppressive. The sparrows, always singularly daring at the Club, continued to raid the tables and fly off with lumps of sugar and bits of cake, but higher up, overhead, MIGs whizzed by in formation. People in the streets would look up and then look at one another.

Russia backed Egypt. She had never had it so good, for, unlike Britain and France, she did not represent a colonial power in the eyes of the Arab world.

Most of our British friends had left, as well as the French and other European nationals. They had been advised to get out of Egypt if they had no urgent business there and to go while the going was good. The British remembered the January, 1952, riots and the Turf Club incidents, and were taking no chances. The larger companies paid the passage of their employees' families to England, but for most of the British who were told to go, it was a heavy expense. Those, like the Maltese and the Cypriots, who carried British passports but who had spent a lifetime in Egypt, stayed on.

Though she didn't want to be evacuated, Betty May and her children left with the other wives, leaving a lonely Peter behind in the large apartment. Like a great many people,

Betty, too, thought the whole thing would be over in three months' time, and she only took a couple of suitcases with her. It was not the first time the British had been evacuated, and they had always returned.

As we sat and sunbathed on the half-empty Lido, we speculated as to what would happen if President Nasser did not accept the solution proposed by the members of the London Conference. The use of force, or, as it was called, "other means," on the part of the West was not to be excluded.

Looking around me, I was amazed to see the Egyptians, usually so hot-tempered, especially in a crisis, going about their business calmly and with a new sense of responsibility. Certainly they made patriotic speeches exhorting unity in the face of their arch enemy, imperialism, but they also built air-raid shelters and recruited volunteers. Strangely enough, they frequently referred to the way Great Britain tightened her belt during the Second World War.

The oppressive atmosphere of the Suez crisis hung over us and all eyes turned to Cairo when, on September third, the Suez Committee consisting of representatives of Australia, Iran, Sweden, and the United States began talks at the Australian Legation in Zamalek. President Nasser rejected the proposals put to him at the conference, and the negotiations seemed to have reached a deadlock.

On September fourteenth, you could have cut the atmosphere of Cairo with a knife. The hour was approaching when the foreign pilots, on instructions from the Universal Suez Canal Company, would walk out, leaving the Suez Canal traffic, so everyone expected, paralyzed. This would prove to the world that Egypt was incapable of running the Canal on her own.

231

But the next day, to everyone's amazement, the Canal was still passing ships through. The Egyptian and Greek pilots had worked round the clock without a break. President Nasser granted them the Egyptian Order of Merit.

Fathia was so carried away by patriotism that one morning at breakfast she announced, with tears in her eyes, that she was going to join the Women's Liberation Army. She was a unique case, I think, among the group of nannies at the Club. The others merely sobbed that their livelihood had been taken away from them now that all the foreigners had left. The Sudanese servants, too, were very upset at the way things were going. Succar daily made disparaging remarks because he said the tea nowadays—and the Sudanese seem to live on tea—was *zai-el-zift*—lousy.

Abroad, President Nasser was being called by every name under the sun, but in Egypt he was a hero. With the nationalization of the Suez Canal, he had rallied the whole country round him. Undeniably, there was a feeling of revenge against the West, but there was also a very deep-rooted fear and suspicion of imperialism, and imperialism to a people only recently out of the colonial stage was a very real thing.

When did they ever have cause to be thankful to the West for anything, Bill's lawyer friend wanted to know. Hadn't the West withdrawn her offer of financing the Aswan High Dam? But Russia understood, Russia sympathized. Just because Russia sold Egypt arms and wheat, though, didn't mean that Egypt was going Communist. Egypt took what she could where she could.

We settled down into a nice rut and I was beginning to get used to the unnatural tension and to being on the verge of a third world war.

On October 29, I got up as usual and was watching Succar scooping the eggs out of the boiling water with his bare hands, when my eyes fell on the *Egyptian Gazette*, which the newspaper man had thrust under the kitchen door the way he always did. It was several seconds before the full meaning of the printed words registered in the fog of my early-morning brain. The Israelis had invaded Egypt. They were advancing into the Sinai Peninsula. I rushed out of the kitchen and called Bill.

"My God," said Bill as he read the headlines, "that's all we needed."

Nevertheless, that day we still managed to set about our routine fairly normally. Linda went off to her little Franciscan convent school with the new nanny—a Copt by the name of Mary who had been with an English family before they were evacuated—and Bill prepared to take off for the office. He said he would call if he had any news. We had been on stand-by orders for some time.

He had no sooner gone than Madame Marika, the little Greek dressmaker, came round with a couple of dresses that needed fitting.

"Look, Kiria Jacqueline," she suggested, "who knows where we'll all be in a few days time? Why don't I finish these here now, on your machine, eh?"

I said "*ne*" which sounds like "no" but means "yes," and she spent the whole day in the apartment sewing and listening to the news on the radio. I had often heard her air her views on the state of the world and on the way things were moving in Egypt. I thought her viewpoint very typical of the average middle-class European in Egypt. She was pro-West, against Russia, and she liked Americans, though, like many others, she was of the opinion that at diplomacy they were newborn babes compared to the British.

"The English are very clever," she always said, nodding her head wisely. For in spite of Cyprus, she was very pro-British, and her son had fought on a British destroyer during the war. Like a great many of the Europeans who had lived in Egypt all their lives, she was convinced that there was no future left in the country for Europeans. But Madame Marika could not bring herself to leave. She had been happy in Egypt, and though she hadn't made a fortune, she hadn't known want. She had her little Arab servant and her washer-woman, and of course, the beautiful Egyptian climate. "But my son can't find a job," she added. "They prefer to take Egyptians."

During the whole of that day, whenever I looked into the room, she'd say, "tsk, tsk, tsk, I know your husband is American, but it is all the fault of that Meeester Dulles."

By the next day, the Israelis had advanced seventy-five miles into Sinai and to within a mere few miles of the Suez Canal.

Just when we needed it most, our radio gave out, and Bill called from the office to tell me the British and French had delivered a twelve-hour ultimatum to Egypt and Israel: Stop the fighting and withdraw to a distance of ten miles from the Suez Canal or we'll take over. Another note was sent to Egypt asking her to accept temporary occupation by Anglo-French forces of key positions in the Canal as well as the towns of Port-Said, Suez, and Ismailia. Meanwhile, President Eisenhower, who had not been informed of the Anglo-French plans and who was very shocked at the whole thing, appealed

234

to the prime minister of England and France to put a stop to their armed intervention in the crisis.

Americans were now urged to leave Egypt, Syria, Israel, and Jordan. Cairo Airport was then closed, and everyone who could do so rushed down to Alexandria to try and take a ship. It didn't matter where it was heading for as long as it was out of Egypt.

On the morning of Wednesday, October 31, I was waiting for Jane Brown to drop round when the phone rang. It was Jane.

"Sorry I can't come over," she said. "I have three hours to pack and be ready to take the convoy down to Alex. The Sixth Fleet is here and we're being evacuated to Italy."

"Heavens!" I cried.

"You'd better start getting ready, too," she added, "it'll be your turn next. I must say, though, with the Sixth Fleet and all, I now have a wonderful feeling of security. Well, see you in Rome."

Things were moving fast now. President Nasser, who had rejected the ultimatum, said that Egypt would resist foreign intervention. General mobilization had been ordered and even trucks were being requisitioned.

I called Pat Logan. She had heard about the Sixth Fleet but she was still hoping she wouldn't be evacuated. Pat and I decided that even though we didn't want to leave, we had better start putting a few things together.

At a quarter to two, I took the car and went to fetch Bill from the office. As I turned the corner of the Gezira Sporting Club, I came upon the American convoy which was meeting here to go down to Alexandria. The line of cars stretched from the main gate of the Club to roughly the level of the

Anglo-American Hospital, some four hundred yards away. Some of the families were patiently waiting in the cars, which were packed with children and luggage; others were standing about in little groups; but nearly all the faces were familiar. There were embassy secretaries, Point Four personnel, diplomatic couriers, people from CARE, U.N. officials, Hilton Hotel architects, American students. I'd be late for Bill if I stopped to talk to them now. A few Arab children stared at the convoy and I noticed that one man was hitting golf balls on the polo field. I wondered who the character was. He reminded me of Nero.

I was sitting in the apartment having a late tea with Pat Logan when the air-raid siren went off. There was the sound of planes humming, a volley of anti-aircraft fire which made the windows shiver, and the dull sound of bombs dropping quite a distance away. The Anglo-French ultimatum had been carried out. The lights had gone out and I felt my way to the bar and lit the yellow candles which stood in the Chianti bottles on the bar. They had looked good at parties. More bombs.

We sat and talked by the light of the candles while Pat's daughter and Linda played happy little warlike games in the nursery. It was a long raid. It took me back to the days of 1940, except that then the enemy planes had been Italian, and Egypt and Britain had been friends. The sound of bombs dropping far away and the anti-aircraft fire were almost continuous. We went into the dining room, which was in total darkness, and opened the shutters. The street lamps were all out and not a beam of light came from anywhere.

Then, in the direction of Heliopolis, the sky glowed bright red.

"Probably the airport," Pat said.

We went back into the living room and sat quietly, busy with our own thoughts. I thought of Betty May and her children, who had been on the verge of returning to Cairo, and who, with all her casualness, would be worrying herself silly over Peter, who was still here. And what about my own parents, who were in Switzerland, where Father had gone on business, stuck in Europe and unable to get back.

The phone rang. It was Bill.

"Get ready to leave with Linda. You're taking the next convoy to Alex tomorrow."

"What about you?" I asked.

"I don't know yet," Bill answered. "By the way, is Pat with you? Well, tell her to go home and pack. She is leaving too."

"And Hank?" I asked. "No, they need him here."

Pat was upset at having to leave. "Not only do I hate to leave Hank," she explained, "but I hate to leave that little table we got in Hong Kong and the Japanese prints." She left with her daughter to go home and pack, and I put a phone call through to Yvonne. I wanted to ask her to meet us at the Cecil Hotel, where we would be spending the night before boarding the ship. Again I thought of Mother and Father. I could imagine how worried they must be about us. While we were preparing to get out of Egypt, they were no doubt figuring out a way to get back in again. This was their home, and they had everything here.

I didn't feel so bad about being evacuated now, because Bill had called again to say that he had had a cable from the New York office telling him to clear out. It would have been the end if I had been evacuated from the place which had been my home for the best part of my life and Bill had remained behind.

We left the apartment shortly after one-thirty. The sun was pouring into the living room and the fish swam about in and out of the coral, making little water bubbles. Succar, his large moist eyes looking even more pathetic than usual, and Mary the nanny, sobbing noisily, escorted us right down to the street. I hated good-byes. The doorman joined the group and we all shook hands. Succar kept saying that we weren't to worry and that he would look after everything as though we were here. I could well believe it of him. As for Linda, the magic name of the Sixth Fleet had more than made up for the fact that she couldn't take her roomful of toys with her, and while Mary sobbed that she would miss her more than her own child if she had had one, Linda jumped about chanting, "Going on the Sixth Fleet, going on the Sixth Fleet," until I earnestly hoped she would go overboard the Sixth Fleet as well.

Finally we were in the car, loaded with bag and baggage, and waving to Succar and the rotund little nanny and the doorman, who looked very sad and lost standing there on the pavement of Sharia Saraya el Gezira.

We drove to the American Embassy in Garden City, where the convoy was gathering. There were cars all round the block and Egyptians sullenly staring at their occupants. Bill got out and came back a few minutes later with a couple of American flag stickers which he stuck on the front and back windows of the car. And we moved off, escorted by two truckloads of Egyptian police with rifles.

The convoy moved slowly at first as it crossed Kasr-el-Nil Bridge and made for Giza and the Desert Road out by Mena

238

House. Here and there along the way, groups of Egyptians stared in unfriendly silence. But at Giza, they shouted, "Get out, get out," and some threw stones. It seemed unreal and sad to be leaving Egypt that way.

It wasn't long before we were driving along the Desert Road, and suddenly there were far-distant rumblings and the car began to tremble. Linda threw herself round my neck and began to whine.

There were three planes, and at first glance, seeing them make a beeline for the ground, I thought they had been shot down, but they were dive-bombing, zooming up and then down, over and over again. We were going in the direction of an airfield and I sincerely hoped that British bombing was as accurate as it was cracked up to be. It was. The planes were still bombing when we left the airfield area.

It was dark by the time we reached Alexandria, and we were just on the outskirts of the city when there was an air-raid warning and the convoy stopped. It hadn't been so bad being in a moving car with Linda, but now, stopped and in total darkness, she was restless and tired but not in the least inclined to sleep.

Our eyes became accustomed to the dark and we could discern people in galabias standing on either side of the road, looking at the convoy. I heard them muttering "Americani, Americani." Egyptian armored cars and soldiers passed by and the people cheered them. We must have sat in the cars thus for over an hour before the all-clear sounded and we started to move again.

It was about 7:30 P.M. by the time we got into town. It was cool after Cairo and the lobby of the Cecil Hotel looked like the Piccadilly underground at rush hour. Practically all the British, French, and Americans I knew in Egypt were there. There were also masses of people I had never suspected of having British or French passports.

Yvonne and Karim were standing by the desk. We chatted for a while.

"Why don't you come home with us instead of spending the night here?" Karim suggested. Bill and I thought it over and decided it was wiser to stay with the others just in case there was a change of plans. We had to be ready at seven in the morning and it was a long way in the blackout to Yvonne's.

Bill said he would stay in the lobby and see if any of the wives whose husbands hadn't been able to come needed help, and Yvonne, Linda, and I went up to our room. Coming out of the elevator we walked straight into a face from the past. It was tiny, wizened little Mademoiselle Boileau, whom I hadn't seen in at least fifteen years, but who was not the sort of person one forgot easily.

"Yvonne, Jacqueline," she cried in her beautiful sonorous voice, just as she used to when she gave us those memorable French literature lessons at home, "what are you doing here?" What indeed?

Mademoiselle Boileau, an important contributor to our expensive and useless education, had seen to it that we would remember the poems of André Chenier for the rest of our lives. In this respect, the woman was undoubtedly a genius. Her method, really very simple, had consisted of reciting the poems while the three of us and anyone who happened to drop in enacted them.

"La Jeune Tarentine," the story of a beautiful bride who is on her way to her love but gets drowned instead of wed,

240

was my favorite. Mademoiselle Boileau's voice muted itself like La Callas' and her eyes filled with tears when she came to some of the more sentimental passages as though she were reading a letter from a dead lover.

Yvonne as the beautiful bride would be out cold on the floor (really the bottom of the ocean), and the part of the devouring sea monsters would go to Helen, who had a reputation for devouring anything, but I would have to make do with being the heartbroken lover weeping on the shore.

"We still need some more characters," Mademoiselle Boileau would say, and since the house was crawling with them, this was no problem. Enter Maha followed by Mrs. James, who was on her way down anyway, because her sister Mary Elizabeth Ann was on the stage, and the two of them as wood nymphs, mountain nymphs, and every nymph except a nymphomaniac would walk sadly round and round, beating their breasts and wailing "alas." In the interval between "La Jeune Tarentine" and the poem in which Mrs. James was the Muse, which was very good too, Gamal came in with his Turkish coffee. Mademoiselle Boileau always thanked him and said a few nice words to him in such good Arabic that Gamal never failed to turn round and say, "Please, Mazmazell Jacqueline, tell her I don't speak French."

These days were long since gone. I looked at tiny little Mademoiselle Boileau. She must be at least seventy-five, I thought.

"They turned me back off the ship," she said. Her head trembled like a wounded little bird's. "They didn't let me sail. I had my ticket on the Greek ship. My luggage got on board. It's gone, but I'm here. No French subjects must leave, you see. *Et vous?*" she asked.

241

We told her about the Sixth Fleet.

"How wonderful," she said. "Your government really looks after you. But the French government, what is it to them what happens to a minority of people like us when they have a job to do, and when they compare us to the whole of the population of France? But I shall complain," she shook her wizened old finger, "I shall complain. I shall write to the *Figaro*. I have a nephew at the *Figaro*."

We asked her if she needed any clothes or money now that she had lost her luggage.

"No, my child," she replied. "I shall go back to my apartment and let *ce cher brave* Hassan"—she pronounced it "Assann"—"look after me. He was in tears when I left the house this morning, wanted me to take him with me. Well, I shall stay home quietly. We are under house arrest, you know."

Yvonne helped me put the exhausted Linda to bed and we went down again to look for Bill and Karim. The lobby was still full of people; we overheard several say that they had been unable to find accommodations. It was like a refugee camp, with tired children all over the place. We spotted some English friends and went over to them. They were all taking things very phlegmatically in typical British fashion.

"What do we do now, Old Boy?" said one.

I had visions of them trying to escape out of the country incognito, with their regimental ties and pink complexions.

"Um, ah, well, ah, how about a drink?" said another.

"Jolly good, it's on sequestered money anyway," said a third. "Very funny" I thought. And they all pushed off to the bar. Just then Bill and Karim appeared and a minute

242

later the air-raid siren went off and the hotel was plunged in darkness.

Almost immediately, planes droned overhead. Anti-aircraft fire burst out, and down came a series of bombs, but this time they were very near, not from a distance as in Cairo. The Cecil Hotel overlooked the East harbor and the Corniche, and though I hadn't a clue as to what it was the British had warned they would bomb tonight, I suspected it might be the main harbor installations a few kilometers away. It occurred to me that Linda would be petrified if she should wake up now with the loud thunder of anti-aircraft guns and find herself alone and in total darkness, and I made my way up three flights of stairs practically on all fours. I heard her howling before I had even reached the third floor, and found her standing in her pajamas with a very wet little face. She was soon asleep, but I didn't go down again.

I do not know exactly how many air raids there were that night, but every time I awoke, I seemed to hear the siren and the whole of the old Cecil quivering with rage. It rained for a while, too, and I slept fitfully. There was another raid shortly before dawn, and I got up, showered, and dressed, by which time Bill and Linda were awake.

We were having breakfast in the first-floor dining room when in burst Maha. She could hardly walk in the high heels to which she was unaccustomed and she wore a bull-red shawl, above which her eyes, thickly outlined with kohl, seemed to stare like something from a Picasso painting.

"It's Maha," she cried, nearly knocking the table over in her eagerness to kiss Linda. "I want her to have my medals of St. Anthony to protect her." St. Anthony and the Sixth Fleet, I thought—what better combination?

243

She helped Linda eat up her breakfast, after which we fetched our suitcases and went downstairs. Yvonne and Karim walked over with us to the parking lot. Little Arab kids clamored for baksheesh. By the car, a group of students glared menacingly, and one of them, putting his hand across his throat and pointing to fair-haired little Linda, said in Arabic, "We'll slit your throats like chickens," and they spat.

We got into the car, Linda, Bill and I. Yvonne and Karim would not be allowed into the harbor area. At the best of times, one needed passes nowadays, and there was no point in their going any further. When it came to good-byes, Yvonne and I were more undemonstrative than the English.

We followed the procession of cars to the harbor gate and stopped just opposite the customs shed. Bill carried the suitcases inside. Then Bill parked the car alongside some others. They would all be taken care of. That was American efficiency for you.

The customs man was dry but polite. He ran his hands through the contents of our suitcases and somebody came along and took them to a bus which in turn would take them to the ships.

The quarantine shed and passports came next, and we stood in line sweltering in the sun, burdened with coats and too many little airline bags. It was slow work, but everything seemed to be proceeding smoothly. Several American Embassy officers were around helping here and there.

At last we had our exit visas, and Bill, Linda, and I got onto a crowded bus and took off. We had gone a few hundred yards or so inside the dock area when the bus stopped and an American sailor opened the door and jumped in.

"Boy, am I glad to see you," cried a woman sitting in the

244

back of the bus. We all turned round and laughed. It was an elderly American tourist, the kind who is always everywhere, seeing everything. I could imagine her regaling the people back home with tales of her trip to Egypt.

"O.K., everybody," the sailor said, "follow me and have your passports ready to show the Egyptian officer."

We filed out one by one and showed our passports to an Egyptian officer and an American from the Embassy, whom we knew. They stood barely a yard apart, as though sieving the passengers.

Hundreds of suitcases were laid on the quayside. I tried to pick out ours and only located two out of the four, but they would all get on board. American efficiency and know-how again. The U.S. ships *Patch* and *Chilton* were only a few hundred yards away and a launch was waiting to take us all aboard in groups. There was still one more control, and we produced our passports again for some Egyptian officers sitting at a long table. There was no hitch and we passed smoothly by. I couldn't believe that I was leaving Egypt this way.

We stepped into the launch. Linda stared at the young marine for all she was worth. Bigger people than she were in awe of the U.S. Sixth Fleet.

The engine throttled up. The launch turned round, and as it did, the salt spray splashed my cheek. As we headed for the ships, the American flag opened wide in the breeze. The American Navy had done a good job, but it had also been a beautifully planned and well carried out evacuation. Neither the British nor the French had had anything to compare with it. For them—I thought of poor old Mademoiselle Boileau— it had been each man for himself. My mind was overflowing.

245

Yvonne, Karim, our home, the things that had been part of me since childhood—who knew when I would see them all again?

Tomorrow, the reaction would set in. Xenophobia, hatred of the West, Communism perhaps, maybe even worse, and I felt sorry for the whole darned mess. As for me personally, the fate which had brought me back to Egypt for a while was sending me out again, but the many memories of the country would remain with me. But now, I thought, I am an American first. Linda and Bill looked proudly at the large gray ships ahead while the old Nile, without whose lifegiving waters all Egypt would be a desert, flowed placidly on to the sea, carrying its burden of cotton bales, feluccas, and dead babies.